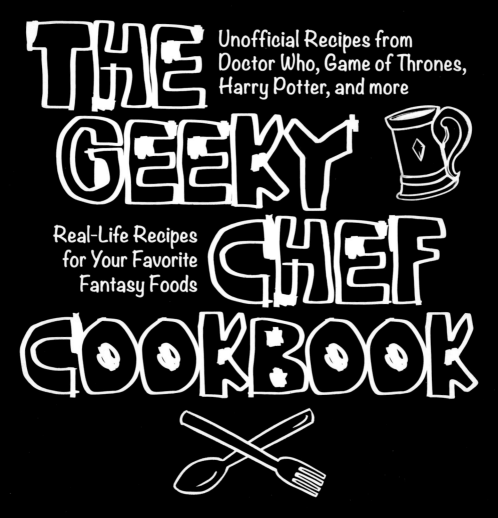

# THE GEEKY CHEF COOKBOOK

Unofficial Recipes from Doctor Who, Game of Thrones, Harry Potter, and more

Real-Life Recipes for Your Favorite Fantasy Foods

Cassandra Reeder, the Geeky Chef

Race Point
PUBLISHING

Quarto is the authority on a wide range of topics.

Quarto educates, entertains and enriches the lives of
our readers—enthusiasts and lovers of hands-on living.

www.quartoknows.com

Dedicated to Gretchen Reeder (1922–2014).
You read me stories and baked me cakes.

Race Point Publishing
A division of Quarto Publishing Group USA Inc.
142 West 36th Street, 4th Floor
New York, New York 10018
quartoknows.com
Visit our blogs at quartoknows.com

RACE POINT PUBLISHING and the distinctive Race Point Publishing logo
are trademarks of Quarto Publishing Group USA Inc.

Photography: Bill Milne
Food and Prop Styling: Noah Rosenbaum
Photo Shoot Art Direction: Heidi North
Illustrations: Denis Caron
Editorial Directors: Jeannine Dillon and Hallie Einhorn
Managing Editor: Erin Canning
Copy Editor: Lindsay Herman
Cover Design: Rosamund Saunders

Cover image (chalkboard) © Shutterstock / Maridav

ISBN: 978-1-63106-049-6

Library of Congress Cataloging-in-Publication data is available

Printed in China

7 9 10 8

# CONTENTS

# INTRODUCTION

So you're a geek, a nerd, a neo-maxi-zoom-dweebie. Or, you know, maybe you don't like labels and you're just really into sci-fi. That's cool. I'm just guessing here, but you probably also like to eat. Great! Then this book is for you.

Generally, the kind of people who acquire the labels listed above, in addition to being wicked smart and perhaps experiencing a certain amount of social discomfort, tend to have a passion for a piece of work that consumes them. My blog, *The Geeky Chef*, was the love child of that intense nerd passion and my fondness for cooking.

Really, I have always had a fascination with food in fiction. When I was six years old, I enlisted my big brother to help me make Tree Star cookies after watching Don Bluth's *The Land Before Time*. I also made Unicorn Hair Soup after reading the wonderful YA novel *Ella Enchanted* when I was slightly older. I could really go on and on with these examples, but the tipping point that inspired *The Geeky Chef* actually started with a *Zelda* game.

It was a dark and stormy winter night in San Francisco. No, really! I'm not making that up for atmosphere. The year was 2008. My then-boyfriend (now fiancé, and soon-to-be husband) and I were playing *The Legend of Zelda: Twilight Princess*. In case you were wondering, we are able to play single-player games together because we have developed a system where I do the puzzles and he fights the bosses, which is not unlike how we handle most obstacles in real life.

The level we were on was called the Snowpeak Ruins, which is basically this giant abandoned mansion occupied by two yetis. To complete this part of the game, Link must collect ingredients to make a soup to heal the female yeti. The ingredients are a fish, a pumpkin, and goat cheese. When you successfully locate all of these items and add them to the soup, you get a consumable called Superb Soup. At that point in time, my fiancé and I had been living almost exclusively on ramen and cereal, so maybe it was malnourishment speaking, but that soup sounded so good to me. I decided as a special treat that I was going to make Yeto's Superb Soup for Thanksgiving.

So I hit up the old search engines looking for a recipe, fully expecting someone to have thought of this already. The game was a couple of years old at that point, but, alas, to my surprise and disappointment, there was nothing. At that time, the Internet wasn't quite what it is now, and though there were some sites with fiction-inspired recipes, they were mostly dedicated to something specific: primarily *Harry Potter* and *The Lord of the Rings*. So I decided that a) I was going to scratch my own itch and make the website I was looking for, and b) I was totally going to make my own recipe for Yeto's Superb Soup. In the end, this worked out pretty well for me.

Now my humble little blog has its own cookbook. This still sorta blows my mind, and I have you guys to thank for it. Thank you to everyone who buys this book, and thank you to every nerd who stumbled on my blog while searching for a Lembas Bread recipe, and thank you for every suggestion that helped me discover new geeky things to love. All of you made one of my biggest dreams come true.

As a little girl I always expected that one day adventure would happen to me—someday a tornado would whisk me away to Oz, or I'd fall down a rabbit hole, or David Bowie would kidnap me and take me to his labyrinth where he'd sing me songs and feed me magic peaches. (I still sorta wish David Bowie would kidnap me, but that's beside the point.) As I get older, I realize you have to make adventure happen for yourself. I hope this cookbook helps you, dear reader, to make some tasty adventures for yourself—and maybe throw some really awesome LARP parties.

And if you happen to be the architect behind any of the works that inspired these recipes: Hi, I love you, please don't sue me! I am a fan, and my goal here is to help other fans enjoy your work even more by giving them a taste of your imagination. I rather hope that this book will help people to discover new geeky things to love, as writing this book has done for me. If you're David Bowie, call the publisher for my address...

# A NOTE ON COOKING AND INGREDIENTS

Cooking is like an adventure: there's an end goal in mind but it is the journey that makes the end meaningful. You'll notice that I leave a lot of room for choices and that some of the ingredients have ranged amounts. This is because I want to encourage you to follow your own instincts when cooking. If you think you need fewer people in your Soylent Green or just a bit more pain and regret in your Pan Galactic Gargle Blaster, try it! Make substitutions, add the ingredients you wish were there, include more of this and less of that. Cooking is rarely a precise science, and it's adding your individual touch that makes the food good.

I guess what I'm saying is play with your food! Experimentation is how you learn and grow. When in doubt, Google it!

Due to the nature of this book, some of the ingredients are a little "out there," as we're dealing in the realms of science fiction and fantasy. I've tried to limit rare ingredients and supplies needed as much as possible. With a few exceptions, most of the ingredients and supplies can be found at any generic grocery store or liquor store. Those that can't, can be found through online vendors.

# BEVERAGES:
## Non-Alcoholic

---

Star Wars: **BLUE MILK**

Dragonriders of Pern: **KLAH**

Various Video Games: **RED POTION**

Harry Potter: **BUTTER BEER**

The Legend of Zelda: **LON LON MILK**

Futurama: **SLURM**

Vampires (in general): **BLOOD**

# INSPIRED BY STAR WARS
# BLUE MILK

Alright, you scruffy-looking nerf herders, this is the most well-known food in the *Star Wars* universe, which, by the way, has a marked lack of canonical food. But I couldn't make a geeky cookbook without including something from *Star Wars*…that would just be wrong. Otherwise known as Bantha Milk or Tatooine Milk, this is the mysterious beverage that Luke Skywalker and his aunt and uncle are seen drinking at breakfast, right before Luke's adventures begin in *Star Wars Episode IV: A New Hope*. The drink has appeared in countless *Star Wars* games, books, and movies since. For more *Star Wars*-inspired recipes, including "Wookie Cookies," check out the official cookbook.

I know this recipe sounds a bit strange, but have you seen a Bantha? They look like a cross between a mammoth, a ram, and a garbage truck. I've seen a lot of *Star Wars* fans trying to get their Luke Skywalker on just by adding blue food coloring to their milk. That's great, but I wanted to take it one step further and make this beverage taste like it could actually be milk from a bizarre creature living in a galaxy far, far away. So, the goat milk gives it a sort of unusual not-the-cow-milk-we-all-know-and-love quality, and the avocado adds some additional protein and thickness. The other ingredients make it palatable—more than palatable. I think it tastes quite nice. Of course, other milks can be substituted if you're vegan/allergic/grossed out by goats.

## SERVES 1

1 cup (235ml) goat's milk (other
   milks can be substituted)
2 tablespoons avocado
2 tablespoons blueberry syrup
1 scoop vanilla ice cream
4–5 drops blue food dye

1 Use the Force to blend all ingredients together. Or a blender.
2 Pour into your cup of choice.
3 Enjoy!

# KLAH

*Dragonriders of Pern* is a series of science-fiction novels written by Anne McCaffrey and occasionally her son, Todd McCaffrey. Pern is the planet on which the series takes place. Periodically, the planet is threatened by Threadfall, which is caused by another rogue planet in the solar system passing close enough to Pern to rain down destructive spores on the planet. The only creatures that can destroy the Thread are genetically engineered sentient dragons that have the ability to teleport through time and space. These dragons come in various sizes and colors and all form a psychic bond with human riders from birth. If you're into dragons and want to see a different take on the mythical creatures, I highly recommend these books. If you're not into dragons, what the hell is wrong with you? Dragons are magnificent!

So, Klah is a hot, invigorating, and spicy drink made from tree bark and is enjoyed by all of the Pernese. It has a pungent, spicy taste with notes of chocolate and cinnamon. It can be taken with some milk or cream, or even liquor. In the world of Pern, people are as addicted to Klah as we are to coffee. They seem to drink it at almost every meal and occasion. Honestly, I'm surprised they don't have a Starbucks equivalent for Klah lattes and Klah frappuccinos... pumpkin spice Klah, decaf iced Klah, non-fat Klah latte with two pumps of caramel, no whip... Okay, I'm done.

## SERVES 1

1 cup (235ml) brewed coffee (instant or made using a machine)
1 ounce (28g) bittersweet dark chocolate
Pinch cayenne powder
Pinch allspice
1 cinnamon stick
Splash of cream and/or liquor to serve (optional)

1 While the coffee is brewing, blast the dark chocolate in the serving cup in the microwave on high for 60 seconds.
2 Add the cayenne and allspice to the melted chocolate in the cup.
3 Pour the hot coffee onto the melted chocolate and spices in the cup.
4 Stir everything together with the cinnamon stick.
5 Enjoy plain or with a splash of cream and/or liquor!

# INSPIRED BY VARIOUS VIDEO GAMES
# RED POTION

The red potion, "health potion," or "healing potion" is a staple in video games, especially RPGs. It has appeared in such video-game giants as *The Legend of Zelda*, *World of Warcraft*, *Diablo*, *Minecraft*, and *Ultima*. Generally, the red-colored potion restores the depleted health of the character that consumes it.

I considered making the potion alcoholic but it seemed to me that it would not be useful for Link or any other character to get sloppy in the middle of fighting evil and saving the world. The taste and consistency of the red potion is unknown as it is rarely, if ever, discussed in any game. All that we know for sure is that it is generally both red and healthy. This recipe uses a multitude of different fruits known for their rich vitamin content and antioxidant properties, as well as a little bit of ginger—which is known to ease muscle pain and acts as an anti-inflammatory—to create a concoction that is very red and will certainly fill up your life bar.

## SERVES 2–3

1 cup (235ml) cranberry apple juice
½ cup (55g) frozen sweet dark cherries
¼ cup (60g) frozen raspberries
¼ cup (40g) cubed watermelon
Handful of frozen mango chunks
1 teaspoon fresh ginger, minced
Red food dye (optional, to enhance color)

1 Put all the ingredients into a blender and blend until smooth.
2 Pour into a potion bottle and enjoy!

# BUTTER BEER

*Harry Potter* is almost universally adored. The release of *The Sorcerer's Stone* in 1997 began a reading revolution among young people, though *Harry Potter*'s charm seems to affect humans of all ages. Harry Potter changed everything, not only in literature but also in the minds of a generation.

Unsurprisingly, the *Harry Potter* series has inspired an unfathomable amount of fan creations, which includes a multitude of tasty wizard treats based on what the characters eat in the books. There is now an official version of this popular *Harry Potter* drink sold at Universal Studios in Florida. It was carefully crafted to J.K. Rowling's specifications and I'm sure it's, well, magical. I hope to try it myself one day! However, for those of us who are unable to make it to Florida any time soon, it'd be nice to whip up some Butter Beer right at home. It is a little known fact that Butter Beer was actually a thing before Rowling ever wrote *Harry Potter*, or really before she was even born. There was a Tudor beverage known as Buttered Beere, which made its first known appearance in writing in *The Good Huswifes Handmaide for the Kitchin*, published in 1594. This recipe combines elements of this ancient Tudor drink, as well as Rowling's butterscotch-y description. And it can be served hot or cold!

## SERVES 2

24 ounces or 3 cups (681ml) non-alcoholic beer (regular beer is great, too)
2 cinnamon sticks
10 whole cloves
10 whole allspice
1 tablespoon imitation butter
1 tablespoon melted butter (optional, for hot version only)

1 tablespoon vanilla extract
½ cup (75g) brown sugar
Evaporated milk, to taste (optional)
Soda water, to taste (optional, for cold version only)
Whipped cream, to serve (optional)

1 Pour the beer into a saucepan and add the cinnamon sticks, cloves, and allspice. Bring to a boil and simmer for 15–20 minutes.

2 Remove the spices and discard the allspice and cloves, but keep the cinnamon sticks for serving if making the hot version.

3 Add the butter flavoring, melted butter (hot version only), vanilla extract, and sugar, and stir into the hot beer.

4 Pour into serving glasses and stir in the evaporated milk (if using) to your taste preferences.

5 If you're serving the Butter Beer chilled, refrigerate the liquid until cold and then pour into a serving cup. You may need to shake it up before pouring if you add evaporated milk. Add your desired amount of soda water to your serving cup and stir.

6 Top with whipped cream, if you like, and for the hot version, serve with the cinnamon sticks!

# INSPIRED BY THE LEGEND OF ZELDA
# LON LON MILK

*Zelda* is a long-running Nintendo series created by Shigeru Miyamoto. The first 3-D *Zelda* game, *Ocarina of Time* (where Lon Lon Milk made its first appearance), is widely considered to be the best game of all time. The *Zelda* recipes I've made for my blog have been some of my favorite creations, and they also seem to be the most popular. Still, whenever I mention possibly making a recipe for Lon Lon Milk, someone always says, "Isn't it just milk?" Boo! Boo to that. Hyrule is a magical land where ocarinas have magical powers and, you know, there are fairies and sentient trees and stuff. Did everyone forget that the cows will have a conversation with you if you play them a song? When's the last time you had a discussion with a dairy cow? I don't think the milk in Hyrule would be "just milk."

Lon Lon Milk is known among Hylians for being very nutritious. When Link drinks it, it restores five hearts. So, I kept this one simple and healthy, but extremely tasty. There's an apple (or apple sauce) to add a multitude of vitamins, frozen yogurt for a protein boost (which helps restore muscle tissue), and some sweet caramel to keep your spirits up. It tastes like liquid caramel apple and will legitimately boost your immune system.

## SERVES 2

1 cup (235ml) milk
1 green apple, cored and
  roughly chopped, or ½ cup
  (122g) applesauce
2–3 scoops vanilla frozen
  yogurt
2 tablespoons caramel sauce

1  Blend all the ingredients together in a blender until smooth.
2  Pour into a glass bottle or other serving cup.
3  Drink half of it in one gulp, wipe your mouth, and let out a satisfied sigh.

# SLURM

*Futurama* is an animated adult comedy TV show created by Matt Groening of *The Simpsons* fame. As the title suggests, the series takes place in the future. The main character, Philip J. Fry, is a present-day pizza delivery guy who becomes cryogenically frozen (by accident) and awakens in the thirty-first century. Though the series is primarily a comedy and can be absurd, it has a strong science-fiction foundation and many geeky references. In addition to appearing in *Futurama*'s opening credits, Slurm is featured prominently in the episodes "Fry and the Slurm Factory" and "The Bots and the Bees."

In "Fry and the Slurm Factory" it becomes clear that Slurm is a wildly popular and addictive soft drink. The drink's actual slogan is: "It's highly addictive!" The beverage is created on the planet Wormulan, where the *Futurama* crew discover that the primary ingredient is, well, really gross. However, Fry is so addicted that he elects not to reveal the beverage's disgusting origins to the world in fear that Slurm will no longer be manufactured. In "The Bots and the Bees," Fry drinks so much of the newest Slurm drink, "Slurm Loco," that he becomes radioactive.

It is not specifically stated what Slurm tastes like, so I made my own delicious Slurm ooze by combining frozen limeade with mint jelly and adding soda water for carbonation.

## SERVES 1

4 tablespoons mint jelly
3 tablespoons limeade, frozen
1 cup (235ml) soda water
Green food dye (optional)
Ice cubes, to serve

1 Blend together the mint jelly and frozen limeade in a blender.
2 Pour the newly made green sludge into the serving cup.
3 Add the soda water and stir until everything is evenly incorporated. If the drink is too strong for your liking, add more soda water and stir again.
4 Enjoy over ice!

# BLOOD

I would guess that many of us have a favorite in the vampire genre, whether it's *Dracula*, *Nosferatu*, *The Vampire Chronicles*, *Buffy the Vampire Slayer*, *True Blood*, or dare I mention the "T" word? Vampires are so present in our fantasies that even stories that are not specifically about vampires have vampire characters. Whether the vampires you subscribe to are vicious killers, tortured souls, infected mutants, or, you know, sparkly teenagers, they all have one thing in common: they drink blood to survive.

Most of us have, at one point or another, tasted our own blood. Blood sort of tastes like a liquid salty penny—it's not great. Vampires, however, seem to experience the taste of blood in an entirely different way to us mortals. My recipe looks an awful lot like the real thing but tastes much better to the human palate. This recipe can be combined with an energy drink (I suggest Red Bull) for an energizing effect, or alcohol (vodka works) for an intoxicating effect, depending on what you're into. Happy, er, blood drinking!

## SERVES 1

¼ cup (60ml) coconut water
2 tablespoons chocolate syrup
½ cup (125g) cherry pie filling
2 teaspoons vanilla extract
Red food dye (however much
  it takes)
1 drop yellow food dye
Pinch of sea salt (optional)

1 Blend all the ingredients together in a blender until smooth.
2 Pour into the serving cup. This can be heated in a microwave or served at room temperature.

# BEVERAGES:
## Alcoholic

A Clockwork Orange: **MOLOKO PLUS**

A Song of Ice and Fire: **HOT SPICED WINE**

Dune: **SPICE BEER**

Battlestar Galactica: **AMBROSIA**

The Dark Tower: **GRAF**

Mass Effect 2: **SERRICE ICE BRANDY**

The Legend of Zelda: **CHATEAU ROMANI**

Firefly: **MUDDER'S MILK**

The Hitchhiker's Guide to the Galaxy: **PAN GALACTIC GARGLE BLASTER**

The Lord of the Rings: **MIRUVOR**

Star Trek: **ROMULAN ALE**

Miscellaneous Geek: **MEAD**

Monkey Island and Other Swashbuckling Tales: **GROG**

# INSPIRED BY A CLOCKWORK ORANGE
# MOLOKO PLUS

Most recognize *A Clockwork Orange* as the highly disturbing film directed by Stanley Kubrick, but it was actually a book first. Kubrick tended to take a book's concept and turn it into something else entirely *(The Shining)*, which was part of his genius, but he didn't always make friends with the esteemed authors whose work he adapted. The film version of *A Clockwork Orange* was nowhere near as divergent as some of Kubrick's other adaptations *(The Shining)*, but it had a different tone to the book. The original novella by Anthony Burgess on which the film was based is violent, and it definitely has a point to make about the nature of morality (perhaps not the same point as the film), but it is first and foremost a dystopian science-fiction story.

In both the book and the film, Moloko Plus is served at the Korova Milkbar. The weird sort of English slang/Russian that the characters all speak is called Nadsat, and "Moloko" is the Nadsat word for milk. Moloko-Plus means milk plus something else; in the book and the movie, "something else" is various drugs. In this recipe, the something else is orange-vanilla vodka, combined with a couple of other ingredients to round it out. The vodka is a tribute to the Russian influence and the orange is, well, obvious.

It tastes like a liquified Creamsicle and will certainly sharpen you and your droogies up for some ultraviolence...which, hopefully, in this case is a game of *Dungeons & Dragons*. Or a knitting circle.

## SERVES 1

¾ cup (175ml) whole milk
2 tablespoons orange vanilla
   vodka
1 tablespoon Irish cream
1 dash of orange extract

1  Pour the milk into a serving glass and add the orange vanilla vodka, Irish cream, and orange extract.
2  Stir and serve.

# HOT SPICED WINE

This little gem is perhaps the most frequently mentioned beverage in the *A Song of Ice and Fire* series, aside from, you know, regular wine. Mulled Wine is beloved by Jeor Mormont, Lord Commander of the Night's Watch, who likes his extra spicy with dried berries and nuts, but without lemon. He considers adding lemon "southron heresy." Mulled Wine seems to be popular among the brothers of the Night's Watch in general, presumably because it helps fight the extreme cold of The Wall.

Mulled Wine is a real thing, of course. There is an ancient German version called Glühwein and a Nordic version called Glögg, but the concept is the same: wine heated with spices and (mostly citrus) fruits. Whether you're a brother of the Night's Watch or you just need something to warm you up during a cold winter night, this is the perfect solution. Brewing this rich and delicious hot beverage makes your whole house smell amazing and drinking it is like taking a warm bath with scented candles...but in your mouth.

## SERVES 8–10

2 oranges
2 bottles dry red wine
1 vanilla pod, sliced lengthwise
2–3 pieces stem ginger (ginger preserves)
4 cinnamon sticks
¼ cup (40g) whole walnuts
¼ cup (34g) raisins
10 cloves
Nutmeg, to taste
Allspice, to taste
¾ cup (180ml) honey, or to taste
5 black peppercorns
1 star anise

1 Remove the zest from the oranges in strips, using a knife or vegetable peeler, and set aside. Juice the oranges into a dutch oven or thick-bottomed pot.

2 Pour the red wine into the pot with the orange juice.

3 Add the orange zest, vanilla pod, ginger, cinnamon sticks, walnuts, raisins, cloves, nutmeg, allspice, honey, peppercorns, and star anise into the pot with the wine. You can also add a bit of the ginger syrup from the stem ginger, if desired.

4 Stir for about a minute to make sure everything is coming together.

5 Cover the pot and heat over medium heat until liquid is hot. Do not boil.

6 Reduce the heat to low and heat for 60–90 minutes, or until flavors are strong enough for your tastes.

7 Once the wine mixture is done, pour it into mugs using a strainer to make sure no spice pieces make it into the serving cups. Can be served with cinnamon sticks. Hodor!

# INSPIRED BY DUNE
# SPICE BEER

*Dune*, the first book in the series of the same name by Frank Herbert, which began in 1965, is the best-selling science-fiction novel of all time. Considered to be the most complex science-fiction series ever written, it has been called the sci-fi equivalent to *The Lord of the Rings*.

The main plotline revolves around a narcotic called Spice Melange, thought to be the most important substance in the Universe. Not like any old drug, Spice Melange grants its users a longer lifespan, heightened awareness, and, occasionally, clairvoyance. The substance only exists on one planet in the known universe, Arrakis, which is also known as Dune. This is a hostile desert planet inhabited by giant worms, and in the series, having control of this planet is tantamount to having control of the Universe.

Spice Melange is supposed to taste a bit like cinnamon and is often used in food and drink, including Spice Beer! In the first book, Spice Beer is the weakness of Duncan Idaho, a much-beloved character in the series, who describes it as the "bes' damn stuff ever tas'ed." This recipe combines your favorite light beer with delicious cinnamon-spice syrup and a shot of Goldschläger for good measure. You'll have blue eyes in no time. THE SPICE MUST FLOW.

## SERVES 1–2

1 cup (235ml) water
4 cinnamon sticks
5 whole allspice
4 tablespoons light brown
  sugar
¼ cup (60ml) Goldschläger
5–9 fluid ounces (150–255ml)
  light beer, chilled

1 Pour the water into a saucepan and add the cinnamon sticks and allspice. Bring the liquid to the boil.

2 Once the liquid is boiling, lower the heat and simmer for 10–15 minutes. The water should turn a light brown.

3 Add the brown sugar, bring back up to a boil, and cook for about 5 minutes, until some of the liquid has evaporated and the mixture has become syrupy.

4 Transfer the syrup into a heatproof container and refrigerate until cold, about 1 hour.

5 When the syrup has chilled, strain out the cinnamon sticks and allspice and pour the liquid into serving cup(s).

6 Pour the Goldschläger into the serving cup(s) and stir. Add 5 ounces (150ml) of the beer into the cup(s) at first, stir, and then taste. Add more light beer, if you wish, to suit your own preferences. Enjoy!

# AMBROSIA

We geeks tend to be purists, but I think it's safe to say that this is one of those rare instances when a remake absolutely improved upon the original. In the new version of this classic science-fiction series, the Cylons, a race of androids that we (humans) created to be our slaves and who finally left us alone after years of war and rebellion, come back and destroy 99 percent of all humanity. When humans had last seen the Cylons they looked like scary robots, but when they return they are indistinguishable from humans. They could be anyone. The remade series is powerful, moving, and full of conflicting feelings, moral dilemmas, and dynamic characters.

The series is loaded with heavy ancient-Greek themes, which may be why the most popular alcoholic beverage is called Ambrosia. In Greek mythology, Ambrosia was the name of the food or nectar of the gods. In *BSG*, Ambrosia seems to be a very bright green version of wine. Some assume it is absinthe because of the green color, but it is used much more like wine or champagne. However, the drink does seem to be more potent than either the wine or champagne of Earth.

This recipe combines sparkling wine with pear vodka and elderflower liqueur to create a nectar-like wine that is potent but easy to drink. Human or toaster, I think you'll have a fracking good time drinking this. So say we all!

## SERVES 1

2 drops green food dye
2 tablespoons pear vodka
2 tablespoons elderflower
   liqueur
¾ cup (175ml) sparkling wine,
   chilled

1 Combine the green dye, pear vodka, and elderflower liqueur into the serving cup.
2 Top off with sparkling wine. Cheers!

# GRAF

Stephen King is often acknowledged as a master of horror with classics like *Carrie* and *The Shining*, but some may not realize that he also created an epic fantasy series. Reading *The Dark Tower* may make you question the nature of the universe, change the way you talk, and possibly make you wish you lived in Maine. One of the many mind-blowing things about the series is that it ties together everything Stephen King has ever written. So, if you don't think *The Stand* has anything to do with *Salem's Lot*, you're wrong and you've forgotten the face of your father.

Graf is something people drink in In-World and Mid-World. It is similar to a hard cider or apple beer. It's supposed to be very refreshing and is consumed in great quantities near reaping time. I know a lot of *Tower* junkies have brewed their very own approximation of the drink, but I wanted to make more of a cocktail version, so no one has to break out the yeast and become a brewmaster to enjoy some Graf on this level of the tower. Drink some of this to wash down that Gunslinger Burrito or delicious Tooter Fish Popkin! You'll be pleased with the result—I'll set my watch and warrant on it.

## SERVES 2–4

2 cups (475ml) apple juice
2 cinnamon sticks
2 tablespoons honey
2½ cups (570ml) alcoholic
   ginger beer
2–3 shots of whiskey

1 In a saucepan, combine the apple juice, cinnamon sticks, and honey and bring to a boil over a medium-high heat, stirring occasionally.

2 Reduce the heat to medium-low and simmer, covered, for about 20 minutes.

3 Remove the apple-juice mixture from the heat, pour into a jug, and cool briefly, then transfer to the refrigerator until chilled.

4 When the juice mixture is cold, add the ginger beer and whiskey. Enjoy!

# INSPIRED BY MASS EFFECT 2
# SERRICE ICE BRANDY

Not only is this game backed up by a solid science-fiction universe, BioWare's *Mass Effect* series has pushed the envelope of storytelling in video games. In *Mass Effect 2*, you resume your role as Shepard, who is now a war hero because of the events of the first game, and you are given command of the starship *Normandy SR-2*, a rebuilt and improved version of the *SSV Normandy*. The catch is that you are also now working for the enemy. As Shepard, you have to make many hard choices—like what to sacrifice, who to save, whether to buy a space hamster, and, most importantly, who to get busy with. Food and drink are not a big part of the game, but there are some minor references throughout.

Serrice Ice Brandy is part of a simple side quest that is totally optional but definitely worth completing. Dr. Chakwas, a stately sort of woman who was part of the original *Normandy* crew, also ends up serving on the new *Normandy*. You are able to ask your crew members if they need anything, and what Dr. Chakwas needs is some Serrice Ice Brandy. If you succeed in finding some for her, she'll do you the honor of drinking it with you. You'll both get a little lubricated and you'll see a different side of the good doctor.

The brandy is blue in color and is served in the red-rimmed tumblers that seem to be everywhere in the galaxy.

## SERVES 1

2 tablespoons apricot brandy
3 tablespoons blue curaçao
2 tablespoons Hpnotiq
Lemon-lime soda, for
    topping off
Ice cubes, to serve (optional)

1 Combine the brandy, blue curaçao, and Hpnotiq in the serving glass.
2 Top off with lemon-lime soda. Best served chilled or over ice.

# CHATEAU ROMANI

Okay, I know I said earlier that Link should not drink alcohol because he could get sloppy, but this is the exception. This recipe is one of my favorites from the blog because it is simple yet addictive. Chateau Romani made its first and only appearance in what many consider to be the dark horse of the *Zelda* series, *Majora's Mask*. *Majora's Mask* used to be an undervalued game in the series but has recently gained in recognition. I think this surge in popularity is well deserved; the game is among my all-time favorites in any series. I have spent countless hours following around the people of Clock Town, learning their secrets and fears, but one of my favorite quest-lines involves a certain magical milk beverage.

Chateau Romani is a special kind of milk produced at Romani Ranch. The ranch is located outside of Clock Town and owned by two adorable red-headed sisters who bear a strong resemblance to Malon from *Ocarina of Time*. Chateau Romani is exceptionally pricey, costing a whopping two hundred rupees per bottle. It's also difficult to obtain as it is only sold in the exclusive Milk Bar inside East Clock Town. In the game, you need to complete several different quests in order to get a bottle of Chateau Romani (including saving some very special cows from alien abduction), but it is absolutely worth the trouble. Chateau Romani will fully replenish your heart bar, as well as give you unlimited magic, although it might make you a bit tipsy, like a certain mustachioed circus leader seen moping around in the Milk Bar during their open hours.

## SERVES 1

2 scoops French vanilla
ice cream
Ground cinnamon (optional)
Grated nutmeg (optional)
2 shots Irish cream
1 cup (235ml) milk
¼ cup (60ml) soda water

1  Make sure all your liquid ingredients are properly chilled before you start.

2  Partially melt the ice cream in a microwave-safe container—you don't want the ice cream to be completely liquid, so make sure there are still some frozen lumps.

3  If you want to add cinnamon and/or nutmeg, now is the time: mix it into the ice cream itself because the fat from the cream will prevent the spices from clumping. Stir the ice cream so it's smooth and lump-free and all the spices are thoroughly mixed in.

4  Add the ice cream to your serving cup. Pour in the Irish cream, then the milk, followed by the soda water. Stir. Note: This drink is not a precise science; levels of each ingredient can be adjusted to fit your individual tastes. So if you wanna add a little more Irish cream in that sucker... Enjoy!

# INSPIRED BY FIREFLY
# MUDDER'S MILK

Fellow Browncoats, let's have a moment of silence for *Firefly*.

The cancellation of *Firefly* was one of the most devastating losses in geek television. Sadly, after only fifteen magnificent episodes, it was taken off the air. *Firefly* was a sci-fi western fusion, created by Joss Whedon. Set about five hundred years in the future, after humans had just arrived in a new star system, the series had a sort of a futuristic Wild West atmosphere and took "the final frontier" very literally. The story followed a group of nine renegades, all with very diverse backgrounds, struggling to survive on a Firefly-class starship. Let's keep the memory of *Firefly* alive with some good ol' Mudder's Milk!

Mudder's Milk appeared in the episode "Jaynestown." It was used on a remote planet called Higgin's Moon to simultaneously feed the laborers, or Mudders (as mud was the planet's only export), and keep them submissive. It has, according to planetary legend Jayne, "all the protein, vitamins, and carbs of your grandma's best turkey dinner, plus 15 percent alcohol." From this description, I imagined it being a sort of alcoholic protein shake. This recipe is not going to be everyone's cup of companion tea but that's how it is supposed to be. I think it tastes pretty rutting good myself. It would be a great meal replacement for one of those days. Fun fact: As a shout out to *Firefly*, Mudder's Milk was added as a consumable item in *World of Warcraft*.

## SERVES 1

2–3 shots of honey whiskey
½ cup (120ml) milk
½ cup (120g) plain Greek
   yogurt
1 banana
2 tablespoons peanut butter
¼ cup (60g) oatmeal
Honey, to taste
Ground cinnamon, to taste
Ice

1 Combine all the ingredients in a blender and then blend until the consistency is smooth and drinkable.
2 Pour into a mug and enjoy!

# INSPIRED BY THE HITCHHIKER'S GUIDE TO THE GALAXY
# PAN GALACTIC GARGLE BLASTER

Douglas Adams' hilarious sci-fi series is legendary. The story began in 1978 as a BBC radio show, and then it became a critically acclaimed series of books. Since then there has been a full-length movie, multiple comics, video games, and countless other adaptations of the beloved series. It has been referenced in everything from *Doctor Who* to the Google search page. The prominent theme is *The Guide*, which is sort of a travel guide for the Milky Way Galaxy complete with hot tips and dire warnings. The Pan Galactic Gargle Blaster, described in *The Guide* as the best drink in existence, was invented by Zaphod Beeblebrox—the flamboyant, two-headed anti-hero of the series.

As Adams has stated, a true and authentic PGGB cannot be made on Earth, as the laws of physics prevent it; however, I thought I'd try my hand at making something relatively close. I might not always know where my towel is but, I assure you, this drink is both expensive and bad for the head. Ol' Janx Spirit is substituted with rum because rum is one of the few Earth spirits that is made from juice. Santraginean seawater is now sparkling water. Arcturan Mega-Gin cubes are a combination of ice cubes and Bombay Sapphire. The bubbling effect of Fallian Marsh Gas was already taken care of with the carbon dioxide gas in the sparkling water, but I approximated the flavor of it to be like that of limoncello, as the drink is supposed to have a… lemon-y effect. Qualactin Hypermint extract? Easy, mint extract. Tooth of an Algolian Suntiger is a sugar cube with pepper vodka to add heat. Mysterious Zamphour is lemon-flavored sugar because, you know, it sprinkles. The olive is pretty self explanatory.

The final result is like a spicy, lightly sweet, lemon martini. It seems mostly harmless while you're drinking it, but it will lay you out so much, you'll think you were, well, hit in the head by a slice of lemon wrapped around a large gold brick.

## SERVES 1

½ cup (120ml) sparkling water
2 tablespoons gold rum
3 tablespoons Bombay
    Sapphire gin
3 small ice cubes
¼ cup (60ml) limoncello
1 tiny drop mint extract
2 tablespoons pepper vodka
1 sugar cube
Green food dye (optional,
    for color)
1 pinch lemon-flavored sugar
    (make your own by combining
    lemon zest and sugar, or buy
    at a liquor store)
1 Spanish olive

1  Pour the sparkling water into a serving cup and add the rum.

2  Add the gin and ice cubes and then the limoncello.

3  Squeeze in a tiny drop of mint extract.

4  Add the pepper vodka then drop in a sugar cube and watch it dissolve.

5  Stir in the green food dye, if using.

6  Sprinkle lemon-flavored sugar over the drink and garnish with an olive.

8  Drink...but...very carefully...

# MIRUVOR

*The Lord of the Rings* is the single most influential fantasy series of all time. Like many nerds, it was my first epic fantasy love. I want to do right by *Lord of the Rings* fans everywhere, especially the fans who occupied the AOL *Lord of the Rings* chatrooms in the early 2000s. Hi, guys! Remember me? I'm the one who never said anything and just hung around like a creep.

Miruvor is the cordial beverage of Rivendell. In *The Fellowship of the Ring*, a flask of Miruvor is given to Gandalf by Elrond after the first council and helps the Fellowship survive the very nippy trip to Moria. Miruvor is known for its warming and rejuvenating qualities. The word comes from the Quenya Lexicon and means "drink of the Valar." It is described as a clear liquid with a pleasant fragrance. It was a bit challenging to create a drink based on these facts, but I hope you'll enjoy this lovely ethereal beverage. The white tea is hot and invigorating, the elderflower liqueur and rose water add a floral quality, and the peach schnapps adds a nectar-like sweetness. The end result is somehow both soothing and energizing. Visually, it is mostly clear but has a light golden shine which I think adds a bit of elven magic.

## SERVES 1

1 cup (235ml) hot water
1 bag white tea
2 shots elderflower liqueur
1 shot peach schnapps
1 teaspoon honey
5 drops rose or orange
  flower water

1 Brew the white tea in the hot water for a few seconds. Do not let it steep for too long—the flavor should be light and subtle and the color very pale.

2 Add all the other ingredients and stir to combine.

3 Adjust to taste.

# INSPIRED BY STAR TREK
# ROMULAN ALE

*Star Trek* is the most popular science-fiction creation of all time. If you're about to say anything or even think anything about *Star Wars* right now: shhh, stop. *Star Wars* is not hard science fiction, it's a space opera. Okay, yes, technically space opera is a sub-genre of science fiction, but still, it's like comparing GWAR to Fleetwood Mac. I'm not implying that either is better than the other, just that they are not comparable.

Now that that's out of the way, let's talk Romulan Ale. This alcoholic drink made an appearance as far back as the original series and was even in the classic *Star Trek* film *The Wrath of Khan*. Romulan Ale has a characteristic bright blue color, though the shade of blue does vary throughout the series. Little is known about the taste of the drink, but what is known is that it's extremely potent and causes some killer hangovers. Romulans are sort of reoccurring "villains" in *Star Trek*—they have never really been on good terms with The Federation—so Romulan Ale is illegal…though its outlaw status might also have something to with the hangovers. What I created is bright blue and tastes kinda like a chocolate orange. It has a nice sweet-and-sour thing going on, just like the Romulans. It's also really easy to drink. I hope you enjoy it, because you won't enjoy it so much tomorrow!

## SERVES 1

2 tablespoons blue curaçao
2 tablespoons rum (151 proof)
2 tablespoons crème de cacao
Ice
Blue cream soda, to taste

1  Poor all the ingredients, except the cream soda, into an ice-filled cup of your choice and stir.
2  Top off the drink with as much cream soda as you desire.

# MISCELLANEOUS GEEK
# MEAD

---

Mead is present in many, many geeky things. It has featured in books by such literary giants as J. R. R. Tolkien, George R. R. Martin, and Neil Gaiman. It is especially present in tales of Germanic influence—anything involving Vikings or the Norse pantheon, such as *Beowulf*, *Skyrim*, and the Thor comics. In Norse mythology, Mead is served in Valhalla, which is sort of like Viking heaven, and the home of the Norse all-father god, Odin.

Food historians have mostly been in consensus that Mead was the first alcoholic beverage ever created. So, what is it? Mead is a type of wine fermented from honey instead of grapes and frequently flavored with fruits and spices. It generally has a light golden color.

Here's the thing: A proper Mead takes weeks or even months to come of age and requires a good amount of expensive wine-making and fermentation supplies to boot. Sure, there are quick and dirty ways to make a sort of mead hooch, but I wouldn't want to attempt it. There are plenty of wonderful recipes out there if you think you want to take on alcohol-making from scratch, but I can't be your guide on that journey because, frankly, I wouldn't know what I was talking about.

So here is my recipe for a Mead cocktail—made with wine, honey, fruit essences, and spices. Put on your helm and faux furs and drink like a Viking! To Valhalla!

## SERVES 5–6

3–5 tablespoons honey
1¼–1½ cups (300–350ml) dry white wine
5 drops orange bitters
2 tablespoons apple cider vinegar
3 whole allspice
Ice (optional)

1 Microwave the honey in a microwaveable jug on high for 30 seconds.
2 Pour in the white wine and stir until the honey is completely dissolved.
3 Add the bitters, vinegar, and whole allspice.
4 Chill in the refrigerator until ready to serve.
5 Remove the allspice before serving. Serve chilled or with some ice.

# GROG

*Monkey Island* was the first video game I fell in love with. With a lot of trial and error and the help of my big brother, I managed to play the game before I could even read. *The Secret of Monkey Island* is beautiful, challenging, and hilarious. It follows the adventures of an aspiring pirate named Guybrush Threepwood as he gets in over his head with piranha poodles, ghost pirates, and health-conscious cannibals. At the beginning of the game, you are told how to become a pirate (because in *Monkey Island* becoming a pirate is sort of like a club or fraternity and there are certain hazing rituals you must overcome) and, in addition to treasure hunting, sword fighting, and thievery, there is one other requirement to being considered a true pirate: Grog-swilling!

The ingredients of Grog listed in *Monkey Island* are not true to life. They're also not appealing or safe in any way. Seriously, the only acids that should be in your grog are ascorbic and citric. Grog is a real drink that was invented by the English Royal Navy for the very practical purposes of watering down the alcohol rations that were given to sailors. This was done because it was common for sailors to save up their rum rations for the purposes of getting totally and completely drunk, which was very problematic. So, originally, Grog was just watered-down rum, but it evolved over time to include fruit juices, sweeteners, and spices. The pirate version of Grog is actually called Bumbo and was considerably more elaborate than the naval version. My take on the drink is a delicious punch with honey, cinnamon, and both tropical and citrus juices. With all of the vitamin C in this drink, you'll be unlikely to get scurvy!

*cont.*

**SERVES ABOUT 10**

½ cup (120ml) honey,
    or to taste
2 cups (475ml) dark rum,
    or more
1 cup (235ml) water
1 cup (235ml) grapefruit juice
1 cup (235ml) orange juice
1 cup (235ml) pineapple juice
5 cinnamon sticks, or to taste
2 whole nutmegs
1 cup (235ml) blue curaçao
    (for a green color,
    optional)
A few drops of green food
    dye (optional)
Sea salt, to taste (optional)
Lime wedges, to serve

1 Heat the honey in a microwaveable bowl in the microwave on high for 20–30 seconds, or until loosened.

2 Put all the ingredients in a punch bowl with the loosened honey and stir everything together until thoroughly incorporated.

Note: If adding blue curaçao and/or green food dye, add a little at a time until you get the right color—more or less may be needed depending on your color preferences. If adding sea salt, also add a pinch at a time and taste until you think it is right.

3 Chill the mixture before serving. This also allows time for the cinnamon and nutmeg to steep.

4 Garnish each serving cup with a wedge of lime. Do not serve in pewter mugs!

# SNACKS and APPETIZERS

---

Discworld: **FIGGINS**

Babylon 5: **SPOO**

The Lord of the Rings: **CRAM**

Doctor Who: **FISH FINGERS AND CUSTARD**

Futurama: **POPPLERS**

The Elder Scrolls: **ELSWEYR FONDUE**

The Hunger Games: **CHEESE BUNS**

The Lord of the Rings: **LEMBAS**

Soylent Green: **SOYLENT GREEN**

Serenity: **FRUITY OATY BARS**

Earthbound: **PEANUT CHEESE BARS**

# INSPIRED BY DISCWORLD
# FIGGINS

Terry Pratchett's wacky and hilarious series contains a lot of edible things, though many are not entirely appealing. Pig's ear soup, anyone? How about some rat fruit? No? But if you're a *Discworld* fan, I highly recommend purchasing *Nanny Ogg's Cookbook*.

Other than a mysterious word for an unknown body part from which one would not want to be hung, a Figgin is defined in *Guards! Guards!* as a shortcrust pastry containing raisins or, alternately, in *Interesting Times* as a small bun with currants in it. I made a *Guards! Guards!* version. I also included figs, because, you know, FIG-gins.

## MAKES 9 FIGGINS

### For the dough

1 cup or 2 sticks (225g)
   butter, divided
2 cups (240g) flour
Ice water

### For the filling

¾ cup (110g) raisins
¼ cup (35g) dried figs,
   chopped
½ cup (120ml) orange juice
¼ cup (60ml) honey, or
   to taste
1 teaspoon orange zest
1 teaspoon allspice
1 teaspoon ground cinnamon
Pinch of ground ginger

1  In a large mixing bowl, add the flour with ¾ cup or 1½ sticks (170g) of the butter. Using your fingers, work the butter into the flour until you have a crumbly texture. Add a tiny amount of ice water to the flour and butter and combine until the dough is very stiff.

2  Cover the dough and place in the fridge while you make the filling.

3  Put the raisins, figs, orange juice, honey, zest, spices, and the remaining ¼ cup or ½ stick (57g) of butter into a saucepan and simmer for 10–15 minutes. If any liquid remains, discard it. Leave to cool.

4  Preheat the oven to 375°F (190°C). Divide the dough into nine even pieces. Roll out each piece until it is ⅛ inch (3 mm) thick, then use a tea saucer as a template and cut around it with a knife.

5  Spoon about a tablespoon of the filling into the center of the circle, then pull the dough edges into the center of the circle over the filling and press together. Note: Wet your fingers slightly with cold milk or water when doing this to ensure the edges seal.

6  When sealed, use your hands or a roller to flatten the Figgin a bit.

7  Flip the Figgin over so that the sealed side is on the bottom. Cut slits into the center to vent.

8  Place the Figgin, sealed side down, on a parchment-lined baking sheet.

9  Repeat steps 6–9 until you have nine Figgins on the baking sheet.

10 Bake for 20 minutes, or until golden brown.

# SPOO

*Babylon 5* is a space-opera series that ran for five years in the 1990s. The series features a good amount of strange alien foods, but the most intriguing (and perhaps the most disgusting) is Spoo. Spoo ("Oops" spelled backwards) actually makes its first appearance before *Babylon 5*, in *She-Ra: Princess of Power*, where it is offered to Skeletor, who quickly rejects it saying that he hates Spoo, even though he doesn't know what it is.

Spoo is made from a type of worm of the same name that is treated with contempt by most of the galaxy due to its annoying habit of sighing all the time. It is considered by many aliens to be the tastiest food in the galaxy; however, it doesn't seem to appeal to human tastes. Or Skeletor's.

**SERVES 10**

1 cup (50g) panko
    breadcrumbs
¾ cup (175ml) buttermilk
1 packet (¼oz/7g) flavorless
    gelatin
3 tablespoons cold water
½ cup (40g) Parmesan cheese,
    shredded
1 pound (450g) ground turkey
1 egg, lightly beaten
6 cloves garlic, minced
2 tablespoons onion powder
½ tablespoon powdered
    chicken bouillon
Salt and pepper, to taste
Blue food dye (optional)

1 In a large mixing bowl, combine the panko and buttermilk and set aside for about 10 minutes to form a panade (bread paste). In another bowl, combine the gelatin and water, stir, and set aside for 10 minutes to allow the gelatin to stiffen a bit.

2 Preheat the oven to 400°F (200°C).

3 Add all the other ingredients to the panko and buttermilk in the large mixing bowl and tip in the gelatin and its water. Mix everything together thoroughly.

4 Line a loaf tin with parchment paper and pour in the Spoo, smoothing the top.

5 Bake for 45 minutes, or until the center of the Spoo reaches at least 165°F (75°C). This is very important! There is poultry in this dish, which is dangerous to consume raw.

6 Remove the Spoo from the oven and leave to cool and set for about 10 minutes. There will probably be a brown layer on top that will be removed later for aesthetic reasons, and a good amount of juice will escape and look very gross, but, trust me, it will taste good.

7 Use a knife to cut the loaf into cubes, removing the browned top from each, and serve! I like to skewer my chunks onto little toothpicks.

# INSPIRED BY THE LORD OF THE RINGS
# CRAM

I get a surprising amount of requests for Cram, the characteristically unexciting biscuit-like food from *The Lord of the Rings*, which is testament to the dedication for which Tolkien fans are renowned. Cram is so unexciting that in *The Hobbit* Tolkien describes eating it as a "chewing exercise." Its few redeeming qualities are that it is so dry that it keeps indefinitely and that it provides adequate sustenance. This food is not to be confused with Cram from *Fallout*, which is a play on the canned mystery meat that is Spam.

This recipe is for a very dry cookie or biscuit that has protein powder added for sustenance and apple sauce for extra nutrients. Additional sugar and apple sauce (1 to 2 tablespoons) can be added to make the biscuit less dry and bland if you're more concerned with taste than you are with accuracy. Enjoy?

**SERVES 5–6**

4 tablespoons vegetable oil, plus extra for greasing
½ cup (40g) instant oats, ground
¼ cup (30g) unflavored whey protein powder
¼ cup (30g) flour
3 tablespoons sugar
Pinch of salt
Pinch of baking powder
1 egg
2 tablespoons apple sauce

1 Preheat the oven to 375°F (190°C).
2 Grease a 9 × 9-inch (23 × 23 cm) baking pan or line it with parchment paper.
3 Stir together the oats, protein powder, flour, sugar, salt, and baking powder.
4 In a separate bowl, whisk together the egg, apple sauce, and oil.
5 Add the wet ingredients to the dry ingredients and stir thoroughly with a wooden spoon.
6 Add the mixture to the greased pan, making sure the batter settles evenly.
7 Bake for 12–15 minutes, or until the Cram is firm and a fork or toothpick inserted into it comes out clean. Cut into squares and serve!

# INSPIRED BY DOCTOR WHO
# FISH FINGERS AND CUSTARD

———◇———

Fish Fingers and Custard became a thing when the eleventh incarnation of the Doctor first regenerated outside of the home of a young Amelia Pond. His regeneration made him very hungry but, having a whole new body, he had no idea what sort of food tasted good to his new taste buds. So he enlisted the help of his new red-headed pal to help him find out what he liked. After rejecting a multitude of different foods, he found something that he liked. Yep, fish fingers dipped in custard.

Let's face it, the idea is meant to be sort of strange and unappealing. In the scene, Matt Smith himself is actually eating breaded coconut cakes dipped in custard. Since making the recipe, though, a lot of Whovians have told me that plain old store-bought fish fingers and regular vanilla custard actually taste pretty okay. I'll take their word for it and bless them all for their dedication...but I wanted to make something that everyone could get down with.

My recipe pairs a panko- and coconut-battered fried fish finger (coconut added as tribute to the reality of the scene) and tangy lemon and honey mustard dipping sauce (that basically looks like custard) which complements it perfectly.

## SERVES 4–6

### For the fish fingers
½ cup (60g) flour
Salt and pepper, to taste
2 eggs
1 tablespoon milk
1 cup (50g) panko breadcrumbs
1 cup (70g) coconut flakes
1 pound (453g) tilapia filets, cut into 1-inch (2.5-cm) strips (cod or haddock will also work)
Oil, for frying

### For the "custard"
½ cup (115g) mayonnaise
2 tablespoons yellow mustard (prepared)
1 tablespoon Dijon mustard
2 tablespoons honey
1 tablespoon lemon juice
2 cloves garlic, minced

1 Combine the flour, salt, and pepper in a shallow bowl.

2 Beat the eggs with the milk in another shallow bowl.

3 Mix the breadcrumbs and coconut in a third shallow bowl.

4 Coat each fish strip in the seasoned flour, dip them into the egg mixture, and then roll in the panko and coconut mixture. Set aside until ready to cook.

5 Heat ½ inch (1.25 cm) of oil in a large skillet over medium-high heat.

6 In small batches, fry the fish sticks until golden brown, about 2 minutes per side. Drain on a paper towel–lined plate.

7 To make the custard sauce, simply combine all the ingredients and mix thoroughly.

8 Liberally dip the fish fingers in the custard sauce and enjoy!

# INSPIRED BY FUTURAMA
# POPPLERS

Popplers appeared in the Season 2 episode "The Problem with Popplers," which is a play on the classic *Star Trek* episode "The Trouble with Tribbles." In the *Futurama* episode, the crew is running low on food supplies and goes to the nearest planet to see if they can find something edible. Lela stumbles upon a pit of edible creatures that turn out to be both delicious and addictive. They bring a large cargo of the irresistible snacks back to civilization, where they name them Popplers, and they quickly become a sensation. They look exactly like deep-fried shrimp and are eventually sold at Fishy Joe's restaurant. Wash them down with some Slurm!

## SERVES 5–7

1 cup (240g) buttermilk
2 eggs
1 pound (450g) medium
  shrimp, cleaned, peeled,
  and tails removed
2 cups (250g) flour, divided
1 cup (50g) panko
  breadcrumbs
1 tablespoon onion powder
1 tablespoon garlic powder
1 tablespoon old bay seasoning
Salt and pepper, to taste
Cayenne pepper, to taste
Canola oil, for deep-frying
Dipping sauces (optional)

1 In a small mixing bowl, thoroughly whisk together the buttermilk and eggs. Add the shrimp to buttermilk/egg mixture and set aside.

2 In a medium mixing bowl, mix together 1 cup (125g) of the flour with the panko and seasonings. Put the remaining flour in a separate small shallow bowl.

3 Prepare a deep fryer–if you don't have one, fill a heavy-bottomed pot three-quarters full of canola oil. Heat the oil to 370°F (190°C).

4 If you have a fry basket, set it into the pot full of oil or deep fryer. Make sure it is dry before doing so.

5 Remove shrimp from the buttermilk bath and roll in the plain flour until coated. Then, dunk back into the buttermilk/egg bath, remove again and roll into the panko/flour mix until coated. Repeat this for every shrimp. This can be done in batches of 5 or 6 shrimp; you want to fry them in batches of this size because adding too many at once can cause safety issues and reduce the temperature of the oil, which will make the batter soggy.

6 Drop one batch of shrimp into the deep fryer at a time. Remove by carefully lifting the fry basket out of the pot or deep fryer after one or two minutes or when the shrimp are golden and crispy. If you do not have a fry basket, use tongs to remove the shrimp. Be very careful not to get splashed with hot oil! Repeat until all Popplers are fried. Enjoy with a dipping sauce of your choice.

# ELSWEYR FONDUE

*The Elder Scrolls* is a video-game series that is chock-full of delicious-sounding made-up foods, and it was difficult to pin down just the right one to put in this collection. As I have a weakness for cheese, this one stood out. In the world of *Elder Scrolls*, Elsweyr is the home of the Khajiit race, which you may recognize as the big humanoid kitties. Elsweyr Fondue is made with three ingredients: Ale, Eidar cheese, and Moon Sugar. When eaten, it restores a massive amount of magicka.

So, Eidar cheese is very obviously a blue cheese and ale is pretty self-explanatory, but the Moon Sugar is a bit of a question mark. Moon Sugar is an alchemy ingredient in the game that restores magicka, and is also used in the creation of Skooma, an illegal substance. It looks like brown crystals and is said to be made from a cane plant, like regular sugar. It is known to have a narcotic effect, especially on Khajiit, so that reminded me a little of catnip. Though we all love watching our cats act like furry little fools when exposed to the substance, catnip is not something that humans often consume, except, occasionally, as a mildly tranquilizing tea. So I made a catnip tea–infused hard candy (for a crystalized look) and added some mesquite flavor. Admittedly, the Moon Sugar tastes pretty strange by itself but adds a nice smoky sweetness to the fondue. You will definitely have more Moon Sugar than you need for the fondue (the nature of hard candy makes it impossible to make in small batches), so alternatively, if you don't want to end up with a bunch of extra Moon Sugar, you can skip making it all together and just add a pinch of mesquite and regular sugar to the fondue.

Enjoy the fondue with an assortment of veggies, fruits, bread, and meats. Hot tip: It goes especially well with steamed broccoli, apples, crusty bread, and tangy/spicy meats. Sugar and sand, furlicker!

cont.

**SERVES 4**

**For the moon sugar (optional)**

½ cup (120ml) water
3 catnip tea bags
⅓ cup (78ml) corn syrup
2 tablespoons mesquite flavor
2 teaspoons cayenne powder, or to taste
1 tablespoon smoked paprika, or to taste
1 cup (200g) granulated sugar
Confectioners' sugar, for coating

**For the fondue**

1 clove garlic
2 tablespoons butter
½ cup (120ml) ale
1¾ cups or 8 ounces (225g) crumbled blue cheese (your choice)
¾ cup or 6 ounces (175g) cream cheese
2 pieces Moon Sugar, optional
Bite-sized pieces of your favorite fruits, veggies, breads, and meats, for dipping

1  First make the Moon Sugar. Boil the water and brew the 3 tea bags for about 10–15 minutes until a strong concentrate is made. Remove the tea bags, squeezing out any excess liquid, and discard.

2  Pour the brewed catnip tea into a good-quality metal saucepan with a candy thermometer attached along with the corn syrup, spices, and sugar.

3  Heat the mixture until it reaches 300°F (150°C), stirring constantly.

4  Transfer the mixture to a heat-resistant container lined with parchment paper and sprinkle the confectioners' sugar over the top. Let the candy cool and harden.

5  When the candy is hard, use a butter knife to break it into pieces roughly the size of Jolly Ranchers. Coat with more confectioners' sugar if desired. The end product should look a bit like sea glass. You will have much more than needed for the Fondue, so you can either discard the excess or crush it up and use it as a rub for meat.

6  Next, make the Fondue. Cut the garlic clove in half and rub the cut sides around the inside of a fondue pot. When done, leave the garlic in the pot.

7  Add the butter to the pot and turn the heat on the fondue machine to 200°F (95°C). Let the butter melt for a few seconds.

8  Pour the ale into the pot.

9  Begin to slowly add the crumbled blue cheese to the ale and stir in.

10  When the cheese starts to melt, add the cream cheese and stir until the Fondue is smooth.

11  Add the Moon Sugar and stir for about a minute more. The Moon Sugar will melt gradually and infuse the Fondue with a sweet, smoky flavor, but it will not melt completely right away.

12  Dip the sides of your choice into the fondue and enjoy!

# CHEESE BUNS

*The Hunger Games* seems to be really polarizing amongst nerds. There are some who seem to hate it and many more who love it. It might be because the story is often compared to (and even accused of copying) *Battle Royale*. Personally, having read and watched both of these, I think they are completely different stories. And, let's face it, pitting people (even children) against each other in a fight to the death is hardly a new concept. I don't think either is better than the other, but there is one way in which *The Hunger Games* excels over *Battle Royale*: food!

There are a lot of mouthwatering food moments in *The Hunger Games*. *A lot*. The moments are extra delicious as you experience them from the perspective of a character who has been malnourished most of her life. One of the more memorable foods is Katniss' favorite baked good from Peeta's bakery: the Cheese Bun. They are described as buns baked with a layer of cheese on top. Seriously, who doesn't like bread and cheese? Carb + melted cheese = heaven, amiright?

## MAKES 20 BUNS

3 cups (360g) flour, divided
1 packet (¼oz/7g) active dry yeast
1 tablespoon sugar
1 teaspoon salt
¾ cup (88g) shredded sharp cheddar cheese, divided
¾ cup (88g) shredded Gruyère cheese, divided
½ cup (120ml) warm milk
½ cup (120ml) warm water
1½ tablespoons olive oil
Butter, vegetable oil, or nonstick spray, for greasing
3 tablespoons butter, melted

1  Combine 1½ cups (180g) flour, the sugar, salt, and the yeast in a large mixing bowl and thoroughly mix.
2  Toss in ½ cup (58g) of each cheese, add the warm milk, warm water, and the olive oil, and beat for about 2 minutes.
3  Gradually stir in the rest of the flour until you have a soft dough.
4  Tip out the dough onto a floured board and knead until it is elastic and not sticky, adding more flour if necessary.
5  Place in a greased bowl and then flip the dough over to grease the other side. Cover the bowl with plastic wrap. Let the dough rise in a warm environment for approximately 30 minutes.
6  Punch the dough down, cover again, and let rest for 10 more minutes.
7  Cut the dough into 20 pieces and shape each one into a sphere.
8  Dip each ball in melted butter and arrange the balls in two rows in the pan. Cover with a paper towel. Leave to rise in a warm place for about 1 hour, or until the balls have almost reached the top of the pan.

9  Preheat your oven to 375°F (190°C) and grease a small pan.

10  Sprinkle the remaining cheeses over the rolls.

11  Bake on the lower rack of the oven for about 35 minutes, or until the rolls are firm and golden. You can tell they're done when you insert a toothpick and it comes out clean. Allow to cool for 5 minutes, then enjoy.

# LEMBAS

Lembas is the quintessential geeky fictional food. It made its first appearance in Tolkien's *The Fellowship of the Ring*. The flavor of Lembas is never detailed but it is said to be able to fill the belly of a grown man in a few bites, which makes it useful for long journeys. It's also supposed to taste more pleasant than it's non-elvish counterpart, Cram (see page 45). If it were not for Lembas, Frodo and Sam would probably not have survived the extremely perilous journey through Mordor.

This is my second variation on Lembas. The nuts and the protein powder make it extremely filling; they will definitely make you feel like you just ate a big dinner. The citrus zest adds vitamins and the honey makes the bread both fragrant and tasty. They are soft, lightly sweet, and very delicate, so it's somewhat of a surprise when you start to feel like you just ate Thanksgiving dinner. I recently took some with me on a hiking excursion. I pretended I was climbing Mount Doom and kept calling my fiancé "Mr. Frodo." He didn't appreciate it, but the Lembas definitely kept my energy up.

## SERVES 10–15

6 tablespoons olive oil, divided
1½ cups (350ml) warm water
2½ cups (300g) all-purpose flour
1 tablespoon instant yeast
1 cup (120g) unflavored whey protein powder
2 cups macadamia nuts, finely chopped
1 tablespoon orange zest
¾ cup (180ml) honey
1 teaspoon salt
5 drops orange flower water (optional)
Large non-poisonous leaves (optional, banana leaves recommended)

1 Grease a 9 × 13-inch (23 × 33 cm) baking pan and add 3 of the 6 tablespoons of olive oil to the bottom.

2 Combine all of the other ingredients and beat at high speed with an electric mixer for one minute.

3 Transfer the batter into the prepared pan. Cover and let rise at room temperature for 1 hour.

4 While dough is rising, preheat the oven to 375°F (190°C).

5 Bake the bread until it is golden brown, about 25–30 minutes.

6 Remove from the oven, wait 5 minutes, and then turn it out of the pan onto a rack.

7 Cut bread into square pieces, wrap each piece with a leaf, and tie with twine.

# INSPIRED BY SOYLENT GREEN
# SOYLENT GREEN

*Soylent Green* is a dystopian classic. It takes place on a future Earth where almost all of the world's resources have been depleted due to the sheer number of humans occupying the planet. Most of the overwhelming population survives, barely, on rations. Soylent Green is the newest of these rations. It is supposedly made from "high-energy plankton" and is much more nutritious than its predecessors, Soylent Red and Yellow.

Soylent Green appears in the movie as an unremarkable green-colored square. The taste is not described, though it is supposedly tastier than both Red and Yellow. Most people nowadays know the big "secret" of Soylent Green before they even watch the movie. Charlton Heston's dramatic acting at the film's climax is just too much fun to imitate. *SPOILER ALERT* I skipped the people (OMG, people!) and made a delicious cracker using furikake as the "high-energy plankton," cuz, you know, oceans. Turns out that people (and/or high-energy plankton) tastes pretty great dipped in hummus! I know, I know, everything tastes great dipped in hummus.

## SERVES 4

2 cups (60g) fresh spinach
1 egg
½ cup or 1 stick of butter
    (112g), at room temperature
¾ cup (60g) shredded
    Parmesan cheese
½ cup (50g) high-energy
    plankton (furikake)
Garlic powder, to taste
Onion powder, to taste
1½ cups (180g) flour
Yellow food coloring (optional)
Green food coloring (optional)

1 Purée the spinach in a food processor.

2 In a large mixing bowl, combine the puréed spinach, egg, butter, cheese, furikake, and garlic and onion powders. Mix thoroughly.

3 Add the flour and combine to form the dough. If desired, add a few drops of each food coloring into the dough and work it in evenly.

4 Chill the dough in the refrigerator for 1 hour.

5 Preheat the oven to 400°F (200°C) and line a baking sheet with parchment paper. Place a sheet of wax paper on top of a flat surface and, working in batches, place a handful of dough on the wax paper and then place another sheet of wax paper on top. The wax paper will prevent sticking.

6 Use a pastry roller or rolling pin to roll out the dough until it's about ⅛ inch (3 mm) thick.

7 Remove the top sheet of wax paper and use a square cookie cutter, about 3 × 3 inches (7.5 × 7.5 cm) in size, to shape the crackers, setting aside the excess dough to re-roll for the next batch.

8  Place the finished squares on the parchment-lined baking sheet, cover with aluminum foil to prevent browning, and bake for 15–20 minutes, or until crispy. You may need a second baking sheet or to bake them in batches.

9  Let cool before serving.

# FRUITY OATY BARS

Not that anything could ever make the cancellation of *Firefly* okay, but there was, in fact, a movie that dulled a minuscule portion of the grief and suffering. *Serenity* takes place a few months after where *Firefly* left off, and follows the crew of *Serenity* as they try to keep escaped experiment subject River Tam hidden from The Alliance.

In the film, there is a humorously bizarre commercial for a product called Fruity Oaty Bars that actually carries a subliminal signal to seek out River Tam. The bar itself seems to be rainbow colored (though that might just be the wrapper) and presumably tastes of fruit and oats. So I made a super tasty baked goody with oatmeal and dried fruits. Warning: Your mind will be blown and a live octopus might come out of your blouse. Also, keep out of reach of mice. Make a batch of these and pass them around your *Firefly* support group!

## MAKES 12 BARS

2 cups (160g) oats
1 cup (150g) chopped nuts, of your choice
2 cups (300g) dried fruit, of your choice
¼ cup (30g) flour
Pinch of ground cinnamon
Pinch of allspice
½ cup or 1 stick (112g) butter, melted
1 cup (240ml) milk
1 egg
2 tablespoons brown sugar
1 teaspoon vanilla extract
Multiple food coloring colors (optional)

1 Preheat the oven to 350°F (180°C) and line a baking sheet with parchment paper.

2 Stir the dry ingredients—oats, nuts, fruit, flour, and spices—together in one mixing bowl.

3 In another mixing bowl, combine the remaining wet ingredients: butter, milk, egg, brown sugar, and vanilla extract.

4 Thoroughly whisk together the wet ingredients, then add them to the dry mixture and combine, making sure everything is evenly combined.

5 If you're going to dye the bars, separate the mixture evenly into as many different containers as you have colors. Add a few drops of the food coloring to each of the separated batters and mix until the colors are evenly dispersed.

6 Pour everything into the baking sheet, making sure to flatten and even out the batter as much as possible. If you're using dyed batter, pour in one color at a time, starting from one side of the baking sheet and working toward the other, creating a rainbow effect.

7 Bake for 30–40 minutes, or until the top is crispy, but not burnt.

8 Let cool to room temperature, cut into rectangular bars, and serve!

# INSPIRED BY EARTHBOUND
# PEANUT CHEESE BARS

*Earthbound* is a fun and quirky old-school RPG, sort of a mix of a children's television show and a stoner's sci-fi dream fantasy. It also has a really interesting and complex food system, which makes it my kind of game. It was a little difficult to decide which food to include here because there are so many interesting options. For me, and I don't think I'm alone in this, the Peanut Cheese Bar has always stood out the most. Unfortunately (or fortunately, depending on your perspective), Trout Yogurt and Piggy Jelly didn't make the cut.

The Peanut Cheese Bar is the favorite food of the lovable species Mr. Saturn. Besides containing both peanuts and cheese, little is known about the bars other than that they are supposed to taste "pretty yummy" and recover 100 HP. If you're the kind of person who loves to combine salty and sweet, you will love this recipe. I didn't want to shy away from getting a real cheesy flavor, so I used sharp cheddar, but a milder cheese can be used instead. ZOOM!

## MAKES 8 BARS

5 graham crackers
1 tablespoon light brown sugar
⅔ cup (160g) unsalted butter, melted, divided
2 cups (225g) finely shredded cheddar cheese
2 cups (350g) milk chocolate chips
1 cup (235ml) half-and-half
1 tablespoon unsalted butter, melted
½ cup (75g) peanuts
Sprig of parsley (optional)

1 Crush the graham crackers as thoroughly as possible.

2 Add the brown sugar and ⅓ cup (80g) of the melted butter to the crushed crackers and thoroughly mix all the ingredients together.

3 Press the graham cracker mixture firmly onto the bottom of a 6 × 6 inch (15 × 15 cm) parchment-lined container and place it in the fridge to set.

4 In a mixing bowl, combine the shredded cheese and the remaining ⅓ cup (80g) melted butter until a paste-like texture is achieved.

5 Spread and lightly press this cheese paste on top of the set graham cracker layer to create the second layer, then return the container to the fridge.

6 Gently heat the half-and-half on the stove, stirring constantly.

7 Place the chocolate chips in a heatproof mixing bowl and add the hot half-and-half while stirring. Let sit for a few minutes.

8 Add the 1 tablespoon of melted butter to the chocolate mixture and mix thoroughly until smooth.

9 Carefully and evenly spread the chocolate layer over the cheese layer.

10 Sprinkle the peanuts evenly on top of the chocolate layer and gently press them in so they are partially submerged.

11 Return the container to the fridge for about 1 hour.

12 When ready to serve, cut into 8 rectangular pieces.

13 Garnish with a sprig of parsley. Or don't...

# SOUPS and STEWS

---

The Hunger Games: **LAMB STEW WITH PLUMS**

A Song of Ice and Fire: **BOWL O' BROWN**

The Legend of Zelda: **ELIXIR SOUP**

The Legend of Zelda: **YETO'S SUPERB SOUP**

Star Trek: **PLOMEEK SOUP**

World of Warcraft: **DRAGONBREATH CHILI**

# INSPIRED BY THE HUNGER GAMES
# LAMB STEW WITH PLUMS

This is heroine Katniss Everdeen's favorite food from The Capitol and it is an absolutely essential geeky food. In the first book, Katniss describes this stew as "incredible" and even tells Hunger Games host Caesar Flickman that it's what she finds most impressive in The Capitol. I'm with you 100 percent, Katniss. Food FTW. Later in the book, when Katniss and Peeta are slowly starving in a cave, Haymitch sends them a parcel of the stew. The specific flavors of the stew are not described. All that is known is that it contains lamb and dried plums and is sometimes served over wild rice, a combination that Katniss finds "perfect." Not to toot my own horn (toot! toot!), but my version is absolutely delicious and is the perfect meal after a long day of terror and fighting for your life.

## SERVES 5–6

4–6 tablespoons olive oil
3 pounds (1.4kg) bone-in lamb
2 onions, chopped
5 cloves garlic, sliced
6 carrots, roughly chopped
6 stalks celery, roughly chopped
1½ cups whole dried plums
28-ounce (800g) can whole
    peeled tomatoes, halved
1 cup (240ml) dry white wine
1 cup (240ml) beef stock
1 tablespoon fresh chopped
    thyme
2 tablespoons ground cumin
2 tablespoons paprika
Salt and pepper, to taste
Cayenne, to taste
Pistachio nuts, to garnish
    (optional)
Cooked wild rice, to serve
    (optional)

1 Heat 2–3 tablespoons of the olive oil in a pan over a high heat and sear the lamb until it gets a good color and doesn't burn.

2 Sauté the onions and garlic in the remaining olive oil over a medium-high heat until the onions become translucent and soft. Then add the chopped carrots and celery and sauté for another 7 minutes, or until the vegetables begin to soften.

3 Add all the remaining ingredients except the pistachios and wild rice to a soup pot or Dutch oven and stir together, making sure everything is evenly incorporated.

4 Simmer for at least 2 hours, or until the lamb is tender and falling off the bone. You will need to periodically check on it, stir, taste, and adjust the spices, if necessary.

5 When done, remove the bones from the stew and discard. Break up the pieces of lamb with a spoon.

6 Serve over a bed of cooked wild rice.

# INSPIRED BY A SONG OF ICE AND FIRE
# BOWL O' BROWN

There are many, many mouthwatering descriptions of food in George R. R. Martin's epic tale, and one might wonder why I chose the questionable back-alley concoction of King's Landing's poorest folk (that phrase works two ways!) to put in this collection. I'm not sure why, but I think most would agree that it's one of the more memorable dishes in the series. It might be the mystery of what's inside, which frequently includes rats, pigeons, and possibly, in some of the more dubious pot shops, a very unfortunate person. Of course, there are also turnips, barley, carrots, and other humble vegetables. Arya Stark was prone to wolfing down (pun not intended, but I'm happy with it) a nice Bowl o' Brown during her time as a street urchin in King's Landing.

This recipe is definitely flexible; pretty much anything can be added to it. I recommend choosing at least three different kinds of cheap meat that you're not entirely comfortable with, because what's a *ASoIaF/Game of Thrones* recipe without a little discomfort? I used chicken legs, pork chump end, and oxtail and it turned out pretty fantastic. Of course, no meat is turned down, so if that one person that drives you up the wall were to suddenly disappear...*

*Don't kill people; leave the assassination to Arya.

## SERVES 5—6

- 2 pounds (900g) meat(s) of your choice (preferably cheaper cuts with bones)
- Salt and pepper or any seasonings of your choice, to taste
- 6 tablespoons butter, divided
- 1½ large yellow onions, peeled and chopped
- 6 cloves garlic, chopped
- 6 medium mushrooms, sliced
- 2 turnips, peeled and chopped
- 1 large potato, peeled and chopped
- 2 medium carrots, chopped
- 32 ounces or 1 quart (950ml) beef broth
- 16 ounces or 2 cups (475ml) ale
- ¼ cup (60ml) Worcestershire sauce
- ½ cup (100g) uncooked pearl barley
- 1 bay leaf
- 2 tablespoons flour

1  Season the meat with salt and pepper and brown in 3 tablespoons of the butter. Add the browned meat to a slow cooker.

2  In the same pan in which you browned the meat, add the rest of the butter, onions, and garlic and sauté until the onions start to soften and turn translucent.

3  Add the mushrooms and continue to sauté for a couple minutes.

4  Finally, add the turnips, potato, and carrots, and sauté for 5 minutes.

5  Add the sautéed veggies to the slow cooker, then add the beef broth, ale, Worcestershire sauce, barley, bay leaf, salt and pepper, and any other seasonings you want to use.

6  Cook for at least 4 hours on a high heat setting on a slow cooker.

7  Sprinkle a bit of flour into the soup and stir in—this will help thicken it—gradually adding more until you get the desired thickness.

8  Adjust the heat to low and cook for a couple more hours, or until the meat is tender. It gets better the longer it stews!

# ELIXIR SOUP

You can probably see that I like *Zelda* a lot, as it has inspired many of the recipes in this book. So far, Elixir Soup has only appeared in one *Zelda* game, *The Windwaker*. *The Windwaker* is a bit of an underdog in the series because it is stylistically simple in comparison to the critically acclaimed and much-beloved *Ocarina of Time*.

Link receives this soup from his adorable grandmother after healing her illness with a captured fairy. The soup is bright yellow and is described as both healthy and hearty—it fully replenishes Link's life and magic bar and doubles his attack power! I can see why it's his favorite. And unlike other potions in the game, Link smiles when he drinks this.

## SERVES 5–7

6 tablespoons butter
1 yellow onion, chopped
3 cloves garlic, minced
1 pound (450g) yellow
    squash, chopped
2 carrots, chopped
¼ cup (40g) cauliflower,
    chopped
2 turnips, peeled and
    chopped
4 tablespoons lemon juice
1 yellow chili, seeded and
    chopped (optional)
32 ounces or 4 cups (950ml)
    chicken or veggie stock,
    divided
Salt and pepper, to taste
Chives or green onions, finely
    chopped
Yellow food coloring
    (optional)

1 Melt the butter in a large pot over medium-low heat and cook the yellow onion and garlic until softened, around 8–10 minutes.

2 Add the squash, carrots, cauliflower, turnips, lemon juice, chili (if using), and half of the broth and bring to a boil.

3 Reduce the heat, then simmer until the vegetables are very tender, about 20 minutes.

4 Remove from the heat and let cool for about 10 minutes, or until the soup won't burn you.

5 Purée the soup in a blender or food processor until smooth (be careful with hot liquids) and transfer to a saucepan or pot.

6 Season with salt and pepper.

7 Simmer on low until ready to serve, adding more broth until the soup reaches the desired consistency. Add a few drops of the food coloring, if desired.

8 Transfer to your serving vessel (preferably a corked glass bottle) and sprinkle the chopped chives or green onions on the surface of the soup to garnish. Drink it with a smile!

# INSPIRED BY THE LEGEND OF ZELDA
# YETO'S SUPERB SOUP

As mentioned in the foreword, this was the recipe that inspired me to create *Geeky Chef*, so it holds a very dear place in my heart and stomach.

In *Twilight Princess*, Link is told that a monster has been seen around Zora's domain and seems to have an affinity for reekfish, which is a sort of red-colored fish known for its pungent smell. You track down the monster by following the scent of the reekfish into the snowy mountains. Upon finding the "monster," you discover that he is a yeti named Yeto who lives in the Snowpeak Ruins with his wife. The Yeti's wife (Yeta) has fallen ill and the reekfish is needed to go in the soup that will make her feel better. When you arrive in the ruins Yeto prepares the soup's reekfish base, but he wants to add more ingredients to make the soup even better. So he sends you off to perilously retrieve a pumpkin and some goat cheese from a different area of the ruins. There's just something about coming back to the warm kitchen of the icy abandoned ruins where Yeto is brewing a giant cauldron of soup that's very comforting.

This recipe is pretty simple because I wanted the three main ingredients to shine; everything else is just there to complement and enhance. I've revised it slightly from the version that is on the blog, but not much. This is truly one of my favorite soups, and I hope you guys enjoy it as much as I do!

cont.

**SERVES 8–10**

2 pounds (900g) kabocha or
    pumpkin, seeded, peeled,
    and diced
1 medium white onion,
    chopped
5 cloves garlic, cut into
    quarters
¼ cup (50ml) olive oil
4½ cups (1L) fish, chicken,
    or vegetable stock,
    divided
1–2 salmon fillets
Salt and pepper, to taste
½ cup (75g) goat cheese
About 1 cup (240ml) cream
Fresh basil leaves, to taste

1 Preheat the oven to 375°F (190°C).

2 Toss the pumpkin, onion, and garlic in a bowl with a bit of olive oil until they are all coated.

3 Roast the vegetables in the oven on a baking sheet until they are tender, about 45 minutes, and have nice browned edges. Transfer to a soup pot over medium heat.

4 Add 3¾ cups (890ml) of stock to the pot and simmer for up to 45 minutes, or until all the vegetables are fully cooked.

5 Meanwhile, season the salmon fillets with a little salt and pepper and pan-fry until cooked through. Set aside.

6 Transfer the soup to a food processor and blend until smooth—you may need to do this in batches depending on the size of your food processor.

7 Blend in small amounts of the goat cheese along with the cream. Add the remaining stock to the soup until it reaches your preferred thickness.

8 Flake the cooked salmon and add to soup.

9 Tear in a few basil leaves, taste for flavor, and add salt and pepper if needed.

# PLOMEEK SOUP

This is a dish that has appeared throughout most of the *Star Trek* series, dating all the way back to TOS. It is a traditional breakfast dish of the Vulcans, also called Plomeek Broth. In the original series, Christine Chapel serves the soup to Spock during his Pon Farr (sort of like Vulcan mating season—Vulcans become a little psychotic during this time), and Spock throws the bowl at her. There were many references and appearances on the *Enterprise* as the soup seemed to be a favorite of T'Pol.

Vulcans (unlike us illogical humans) eat for practical purposes only, not for pleasure, so most of their food is considered pretty bland and boring by human standards. Vulcans are also vegan by nature so their food does not contain any animal products. Plomeek soup is no different in those regards; however, the soup can be spiced up a bit. On *DS9*, Bashir orders it with a "touch of basil," and on *Voyager*, Neelix makes a version that Tuvok finds to be "too spicy." The soup doesn't seem to have a standard color or consistency, as it appears to look different each time it is shown, making it logical to assume that the dish is flexible. I have made a vegan soup that is simple tasting and nutritious (though probably a little "spicy" by Vulcan standards), served with just a touch of basil. Eat this and you will definitely live long and (maybe) prosper.

## SERVES 8–10

2 tablespoons olive oil
1 leek, chopped
4 tablespoons garlic, minced
1 medium carrot, peeled and chopped
½ cup (38g) lima beans
½ cup (75g) cauliflower florets, chopped
1 cup (150g) peas

64 ounces or 2 quarts (1.8L) vegetable stock
3 medium tomatoes, chopped
1 cup (175g) corn kernels
Salt and pepper, to taste
2 tablespoons fresh parsley, chopped
5 basil leaves, sliced into strips
2 teaspoons lemon juice

1. Heat the olive oil in a large stock pot on medium heat.
2. Add the leek and garlic and cook until the leek begins to soften.
3. Add the carrots, lima beans, cauliflower, and peas and cook for about 5 more minutes, stirring occasionally.
4. Increase the heat to high and add the stock. Bring to a simmer.
5. Once it's simmering, add the tomatoes and corn.
6. Bring heat to low and cook with pot covered until the vegetables are tender enough to pierce easily with a fork, about 30 minutes. Don't overcook.
7. At this point, add the salt and pepper.
8. Remove from the heat and blend together in a food processor—it's a lot of soup so you might need to do it in batches.
9. Add the parsley, basil, and lemon juice right before serving.

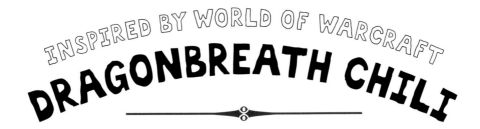

# INSPIRED BY WORLD OF WARCRAFT
# DRAGONBREATH CHILI

I had to include something from the still undefeated champion of MMORPGs, *World of Warcraft*. *WoW* is the MMO version of Blizzard's 1994 hit game *Warcraft*. At the peak of its popularity, the game had over ten million subscribers worldwide. I myself have spent a good deal of my life in Azeroth and I don't regret it. Though the game has a reputation for being addictive and isolating, *WoW* has been an important place for geeks everywhere to gather and build a diverse and vibrant community. Spend, like, ten minutes in Barrens chat and you'll see what I mean.

As players know, there are hundreds of food items in *World of Warcraft*. The reason I chose Dragonbreath Chili is because it has one of the most dramatic food effects in the game. Also, chili is a great food to eat while playing *WoW* because it's easy to reheat, it's versatile, it's nutritious, and your keyboard won't get all greasy—plus, it's easy to reheat. I know pizza tends to be the gaming food of choice, but I'm telling you, chili is where it's at. This recipe is a modified version of my favorite gaming chili, made so hot you'll be breathing fire. The secret ingredient is coffee, which I know sounds kinda weird, but it adds a great depth of flavor and, of course, caffeine. Before you do your dailies, prep the chili and let it roll while you quest—an hour or two later, you'll have some delicious fuel to get you through the grind. I speak from experience.

## SERVES 8–12

1 yellow onion, finely chopped
Butter or oil, for frying
1–2 habenero chilies, seeded and finely chopped
1–2 Jalapeños, seeded and finely chopped
1 poblano chili, seeded and chopped
1 red bell pepper, seeded and chopped
6 cloves garlic, minced
2½ pounds (1.1kg) ground mystery meat (your choice)

¾ cup (180ml) spicy V8 juice
½ cup (120ml) strong brewed coffee
2 ×15.5-ounce (439g) cans red kidney beans, drained
2 × 14.5-ounce (411g) cans diced tomatoes
8-ounce (227g) can tomato sauce
4 tablespoons chili powder
4 tablespoons ground cumin
2 tablespoons onion powder
1 tablespoon smoked paprika
Salt and pepper, to taste

1 Sauté the onion in some butter or oil over a medium-high heat for about 2 minutes. Add the chilies and red pepper and sauté for another 2 minutes. Add the garlic and continue to cook until everything is lightly caramelized, about 5 minutes.

2 In a separate pan, brown the ground mystery meat. Try not to break it up too much while browning if you want bigger pieces of meat in the chili. After it's done browning, drain the excess fat, if necessary.

3 Add the meat to the onions and peppers and mix together.

4 Transfer everything to a stock pot or Dutch oven with all the remaining ingredients and stir together over a high heat for 5 minutes, or until it starts to bubble.

5 Reduce the heat to low and simmer the chili, uncovered, for around 2 hours. Stir and taste periodically to see if you want to add more spices. Chili tends to burn and harden on the base of the pot, so it's good to scrape the bottom with a wooden spoon occasionally.

6 Serve with your favorite chili fixin's.

# ENTRÉES

---

Adventure Time: **BACON PANCAKES**

The Avengers: **SHAWARMA**

Deadly Premonition: **SINNER'S SANDWICH**

Defiance: **BULGAR ASHKHAN**

Star Trek: **HASPERAT**

The Legend of Zelda: **ROCK SIRLOIN**

Pulp Fiction: **BIG KAHUNA BURGER**

Redwall: **DEEPER'N'EVER PIE**

Star Trek: **GAGH**

# BACON PANCAKES

*Adventure Time* is an animated series on Cartoon Network that follows Jake the Dog and Finn the Human in their wacky adventures in the land of Ooo. It began as an animated short that went viral and eventually became its own series. *Adventure Time* makes frequent references to video games, epic fantasies, and other geeky stuff. Though the target audience is primarily children, *Adventure Time* appeals to children and adults alike...especially adults who feel like they are just really tall kids.

One of the many fun and unique things about the show is the music. This particular gem of a recipe comes from a little ditty called, yep, you guessed it, "Bacon Pancakes," written by Rebecca Sugar. It is sung by Jake the Dog during the episode "Burning Low" as he makes breakfast. The concept of bacon pancakes is pretty simple: you take some bacon and put it in a pancake, and then top the cakes off with some maple syrup for a breakfast that is truly mathematical!

## MAKES 10 PANCAKES

10 strips of bacon, fried
    until crispy
1 cup (120g) flour
2 tablespoons sugar
1 teaspoon baking powder
Pinch of baking soda
2 tablespoons butter, melted,
    plus extra for frying
¾ cup (180g) buttermilk
1 egg
Pinch of salt
Maple syrup, to serve

1 Combine the flour, sugar, baking powder, and baking soda in a mixing bowl.
2 In a separate bowl, whisk together the butter and buttermilk, then whisk in the egg.
3 Tip the flour mixture into the buttermilk mixture and whisk together until it is lump-free.
4 Prepare a large skillet by melting some butter to prevent the batter from sticking, then add as many bacon strips as you can put in the skillet with enough distance between each one to add the pancake batter. You will probably have to do this in batches.
5 Pour the pancake batter down the length of each bacon strip until it is covered. Make sure the batter around one bacon strip does not touch the batter covering a neighboring strip of bacon—you want them to be individual pancakes and rectangular-ish.
6 Cook until the pancake batter starts to bubble on the surface, then flip them over and brown the other side. Repeat until there are no more slices of bacon. Drizzle with maple syrup and serve. Defiance.

# INSPIRED BY THE AVENGERS
# SHAWARMA

This one appeared in the 2012 film version of Marvel's beloved comic series *The Avengers*. It's no secret that I love Joss Whedon, because I frequently remind people of this fact. The Shawarma joke actually has an awesome double-geek meaning. At the end of Nicholas Brenden's audition for the role of Xander in *Buffy the Vampire Slayer*, he asked everybody out for Shawarma. Joss Whedon found it hilarious and the gesture may have ultimately landed him the role. Over a decade later, Tony Stark casually invites the rest of the Avengers out for Shawarma after saving New York from an extra-terrestrial invasion. After the film's credits, you can see the exhausted Avengers quietly enjoying a Shawarma together in a local New York joint.

After watching *The Avengers*, I went out and tried some Shawarma from a local eatery and was much delighted. Shawarma is an Arabic meat preparation, involving roasting meats on a vertical spit for hours. Shavings of the meat are cut and stuffed into a pocket of pita bread with various veggies and sauces. Despite not having access to a spit at home, there are a few ways of making a decent homemade Shawarma. Soon you'll be chowing down on some just like Thor in *The Avengers*. Seriously, watch it again. He is loving it.

## SERVES 4–6

### For the chicken

1 pound (450g) boneless
 skinless chicken breast
1 pound (450g) boneless
 skinless chicken thighs
¼ cup (60ml) olive oil
6 cloves garlic, minced
2 teaspoons ground cumin
1 teaspoon curry powder
1 teaspoon paprika
1 teaspoon turmeric
1 teaspoon allspice
Pinch of cayenne pepper
Salt and pepper, to taste

### For the sauce

¾ cup (175g) plain Greek yogurt
½ cup (120g) tahini
4 tablespoons lemon juice
2 cloves garlic, minced
2 green onions, finely chopped
2 teaspoons ground cumin
Salt and pepper, to taste
1–2 tablespoons olive oil,
 for frying

### For the pita

4 large pitas or 8 small pitas
Red onions, thinly sliced,
 to taste
Tomatoes, thinly sliced,
 to taste
Cucumber, thinly sliced,
 to taste

1  Slice the chicken breasts and thighs into 2-inch- (5 cm) thick strips and put in a mixing bowl. Add the olive oil and all of the remaining chicken ingredients and combine, making sure the chicken pieces are evenly coated with oil and spices.

2  Transfer the coated chicken to a zip-top plastic bag and leave to marinate in the fridge for as long as possible—preferably overnight, but for at least 2 hours.

3  Preheat your oven to 400°F (200°C). Place the chicken on an aluminum foil–lined baking sheet and roast for about 15 minutes, turning the pieces over halfway through the cooking time.

4  Remove the chicken from the oven and let it rest for a few minutes. Meanwhile, make the sauce by thoroughly combining all of the sauce ingredients. Set aside.

5  Thinly slice the cooked chicken.

6  Heat the olive oil in a large sauté pan, add the sliced chicken, and sauté until it turns brown and crisp on the edges. Be sure not to overcrowd the pan—you may have to do this in batches. You can add some additional spices (from the chicken section) at this point if you like things spicier.

7  Time to assemble the pita! If desired, grill your pitas lightly for about a minute on each side. Open the pita and evenly spread the sauce inside, then fill the pocket with the chicken, onions, tomatoes, and cucumber to your personal preferences. Enjoy!

# INSPIRED BY DEADLY PREMONITION
# SINNER'S SANDWICH

*Deadly Premonition* is definitely a unique experience. There's a lot of depth and variety to this video game, but there are also a lot of things that don't make sense. The latter adds to the charm for fans of the game…and alienates a good amount of other people. It's been described as a good bad game, and I think that sums it up pretty well.

This sandwich appears in an optional cutscene in the A&G Diner, wherein Harry Stewart stops by to order it while York (the protagonist of the game) and Emily are having lunch. York originally thinks Mr. Stewart is eating this bizarre sandwich to punish himself, but, using rhymes and the frequent repeating of "so says Mr. Stewart," York is persuaded to give it a try. Surprisingly, or maybe unsurprisingly, York loves it.

Eating this sandwich is actually a lot like playing *Deadly Premonition* in that you feel like you shouldn't like it because it doesn't make any sense, but you kinda do anyway because it's strangely addictive. The flavor combination is similar to the iconic Thanksgiving sandwich—similar in much the same way *Deadly Premonition* is similar to *Twin Peaks*—yet it's somehow even more bizarre. I recommend adding a bit of heat for some extra punishment. That seems like a good idea, doesn't it, Zach? My coffee says so.

## MAKES 1 SANDWICH

Spicy chipotle sandwich
  spread or spicy mayo
  (optional)
2 slices white bread
⅛ pound or 2 ounces (50g)
  cooked turkey slices
Arugula, to taste
1–2 slices pepper jack
  cheese
1 tablespoon strawberry jam
¼ cup (7g) Chex cereal

1  Smear the spicy sandwich spread of your choice onto one of the slices of white bread.

2  Top the spread with the turkey slices.

3  Scatter the arugula over the turkey.

4  Place the cheese on top of the arugula.

5  On the other slice of bread, spread the strawberry jam.

6  Press the Chex on top of the jam.

7  At this point, you can choose whether to eat the sandwich with the cereal and jam on top as it appears in most of the cutscenes, or you can face that piece down and enjoy it how it appears when York actually eats it.

8  Atone for your sins.

# INSPIRED BY DEFIANCE
# BULGAR ASHKHAN

*Defiance* is a show on the Syfy network with a corresponding MMORPG. It takes place around thirty years in the future after a bunch of alien races have arrived on Earth and terraformed the entire planet. The story follows the humans and aliens coexisting in a town called Defiance, formerly St. Louis, Missouri. Defiance exists independently of the Earth Republic, which controls the majority of what was once North America. Because the town does not exclude any type, it is a melting pot of alien races, who all bring their own cultural influences, including food.

Bulgar Ashkhan is a traditional dish of the Castithan race—a race who are pale and nice to look at but have a tendency to be arrogant and self-serving. The dish is seen in the season 1 episode "Brothers in Arms" when it is prepared for alien mob boss and quasi-villain Datak Tar. It looks like pink oatmeal but is clearly savory, given the identifiable ingredients shown on the preparation table: red chili, bell pepper, and spices. When I first heard the characters say "Bulgar Ashkhan," I thought they were referring to actual bulgur (the wheat), so I have included that in the ingredients and made a sort of spicy pink curry. No shtako, it is delicious!

## SERVES 5–6

1 red onion, chopped
3 cloves garlic, minced
Butter or oil, for sautéing
1 large red bell pepper, seeded and chopped
1–2 red chilies, seeded and chopped
1 pound (450g) ground pow (pork)
10 fresh basil leaves, whole
2 tablespoons fish sauce
1 cup (180g) bulgur, cooked and drained
2 tablespoons red curry paste
1½ cups (355ml) coconut milk
Beet juice or pink food coloring (for color)

1 In a large pan, sauté the onion and garlic in oil or butter over medium-high heat until the onions are translucent.

2 Add the bell pepper and chili and sauté for 5 more minutes.

3 Add the ground pork, basil, and fish sauce to the veggies and stir to combine, breaking up the pork. Cook until the meat is no longer pink.

4 Tip the cooked bulgur into the pork mixture and combine thoroughly, continuing to sauté on medium–low heat.

5 Stir in the red curry paste—it should evenly coat everything in the pan—then add the coconut milk and stir some more.

6 Let simmer, uncovered, for about 10 minutes. Add the beet juice or food coloring right before you're planning to serve and stir to make sure the color is evenly dispersed.

# INSPIRED BY STAR TREK
# HASPERAT

Hasperat has appeared in three *Star Trek* series: *Voyager*, *TNG*, and most often in *DS9*. It's a traditional Bajoran dish, made from a brine that is known for being spicy enough to make one's eyes water and figuratively set the mouth on fire. I felt the need to clarify "figuratively" because this is *Star Trek* we're talking about—anything can and does happen. Hasperat is mentioned (and eaten) pretty often in *Deep Space 9*, as this particular series takes place in Bajoran territory. It is also a favorite of *TNG*'s Ensign Ro, whose father made an especially strong Hasperat.

Hasperat generally appears as a wrap or burrito and is eaten with the hands. So, this recipe is for a grilled wrap with hot pickled veggies (for the brined element) and hot sauce, complemented by cheese, avocado, and onions. It will make your eyes water and will definitely sear your tongue, but it will be so tasty, you'll happily endure the pain. This makes for a wonderful light lunch or an on-the-go meal to take to the holodeck or on an away mission outside your home after watching *Star Trek* all day.

## MAKES 2 HASPERAT

2 large tortillas
½ cup or 4 ounces (115g)
  cream cheese
Hot sauce (to taste)
½ cup or 2 ounces (55g)
  shredded Monterey
  Jack cheese
¼ avocado, peeled, destoned
  and thinly sliced
½ red onion, chopped
½ cup (70g) hot pickled
  vegetables, chopped
¼ cup (15g) spinach or
  arugula leaves

1  Zap (or phaser) your tortillas in the microwave on high covered with a damp piece of paper towel for a few seconds so they are pliable.

2  In a small bowl, mix the cream cheese with the desired amount of hot sauce. Spread this mixture on your tortillas, making sure to completely cover them—this is what's going to hold the wrap together.

3  Layer the cheese on top, then top with the avocado, onion, spinach or arugula, and hot pickled vegetables.

4  Roll up the tortillas tightly and tuck in the ends. If you wish, you can lightly grill them on each side for a few minutes.

5  Cut each wrap in half diagonally and serve.

# ROCK SIRLOIN

Rock Sirloin or Sirloin Rocks has been mentioned or appeared in three Zelda games: *OoT*, *MM*, and *TP*. It is a "food" item eaten only by the Goron race, whose diet consists solely of rocks. The Rock Sirloin is sort of like the lobster of Goron cuisine: it's fancy. It's only found in Dondongo's Cavern, making it a rare and somewhat dangerous delicacy. In *Majora's Mask*, getting a Rock Sirloin is necessary to obtain one of the game's many masks.

Rock Sirloin appears as rocks in the shape of a cut of meat that only seems to exist in Japanese cartoons. I imagine that Goron's Rock Sirloin is crunchy on the outside and filled with tender earthy/meaty flavor on the inside. So, I made a simplified but incredibly tasty version of a beef Wellington, which is tender beef coated with duxelles and wrapped in a crispy, buttery puff pastry, which just so happens to look like a rock when cooked. The flavor is both earthy and rich. Draw yourself a bath, put on Saria's Song, and pretend you're a Goron luxuriating in a hot spring while eating a delicious Rock Sirloin.

## SERVES 1–2

12 medium mushrooms
4 shallots, peeled and diced
Fresh thyme, to taste, chopped
3 tablespoons butter, divided
Salt and pepper, to taste
¼ cup (60ml) sherry
6 ounces (170g) high-quality steak, cut into two pieces
1 sheet ready-made puff pastry, thawed
2–3 slices prosciutto

1  Preheat the oven to 350°F (180°C).
2  Finely mince the mushrooms in a food processor.
3  Cook the mushrooms, shallots, and thyme in 1 tablespoon of butter with the salt and pepper until they begin to brown.
4  Add another tablespoon of butter and, when melted, add the sherry. Sauté until all the liquid is absorbed, then remove from heat and set aside to cool.
5  Wrap each piece of steak in twine to make a round shape. Season with salt and pepper.
6  In a hot pan over high heat, brown both pieces of steak in 1 tablespoon of butter for 1–1½ minutes on each side. When done, remove the twine and let the meat rest.
7  Unroll the puff pastry sheet and layer on the prosciutto, then the mushroom mixture.

8  In the center of the pastry sheet, place both pieces of meat, side by side.

9  Fold the pastry over the meat to create a figure eight or infinity-type shape. Cut off any excess dough.

10  Bake on a parchment-lined cookie sheet for 15–20 minutes, or until the pastry is a flaky golden brown.

11  Remove from the oven and skewer either end with corn skewers. Enjoy!

# BIG KAHUNA BURGER

Quentin Tarantino's films are not everyone's cup of homicidal tea, but they have a strong cult following and are widely acknowledged for their memorable characters, excellent dialogue, and well-choreographed violence. Personally, I am a huge fan. The fictional burger joint Big Kahuna Burger is mentioned in several of Quentin Tarantino's films, but the most memorable reference occurs in the classic *Pulp Fiction*, in the infamous scene when Jules and Vincent bust in on the unfortunate folks who wronged Marcellus Wallace and proceed to eat their burgers and shoot up the place.

So, Big Kahuna Burger is clearly a HA-waiian-themed burger joint, but what Jules appears to be eating in the scene is a typical fast-food burger. I wanted to reconcile those two things so that the burger would taste Hawaiian but look like the generic burger in the scene. I figured, in true fast-food tradition, to put the differentiating element in the patty itself. The patties are made with pineapple and bacon mixed into the beef and coated in teriyaki sauce. Make sure to eat them before eleven in the morning because hamburgers are, in the immortal words of Jules, the cornerstone of any nutritious breakfast.

## MAKES 6–8 BURGERS

1 pound (450g) ground beef
10 slices bacon, cooked crispy and crumbled
½ red onion, minced
1 egg
20-ounce (567g) can crushed pineapple, thoroughly drained
2 tablespoons bread crumbs

Salt and pepper, to taste
Teriyaki glaze, to coat
6–8 plain hamburger buns
6–8 slices cheddar cheese
Excessive ketchup
Pickles, tomato, onion, and mayo, to serve (optional)
6–8 leaves iceberg lettuce (optional)

1 Heat a grill to medium. You can also use a frying pan over medium-high heat.

2 In a mixing bowl, combine the ground beef, bacon, onion, egg, crushed pineapple, bread crumbs, and salt and pepper.

3 Form 6–8 meat patties from the mixture—their size will depend on how large the buns are.

4 Coat each patty with teriyaki glaze.

5 Grill or fry the patties on both sides to the desired doneness.

6 While the patties are cooking, toast the buns.

7 When the patties are done, glaze each one again with more teriyaki, then top with a slice of cheese.

8 Spread some ketchup over the cheese and place the patties on the bottom bun. Load up with any additional burger toppings you want to use, then finish with some lettuce leaves. Close each burger with the top bun and press down.

9 Use the burger as an effective intimidation technique because you are bad...and wash down with a tasty beverage—like Sprite!

# DEEPER'N'EVER PIE

*Redwall* is one of those series that's just filled with beautiful descriptions of food. Candied chestnuts, dandelion cordials, honey-covered hotcakes, shrimp garnished with cream and rose leaves… I couldn't possibly cover all of it. For more scrumptious *Redwall* recipes from the author himself, Brian Jacques, I recommend also adding *The Official Redwall Cookbook* to your nerdy cookbook collection.

Deeper'n'Ever Pie's full title is Deeper'n'Ever Turnip'n'Tater'n'Beetroot Pie. So, for some context, the characters in the *Redwall* series are all anthropomorphic animals (primarily woodland creatures) with cultures, dialects, and dispositions that are determined by animal type. This pie is the favorite dish of the moles, who unsurprisingly enjoy root vegetables. I added cheese and herbs to make a delicious and earthy pie that will hopefully make the moles say, "Boi 'eck, oi loik dis pie, yes zurr! Quoite noice, says oi!"

## MAKES 2 PIES

### For the crust

2 cups (240g) all-purpose flour
Pinch of salt
¼ cup or ½ stick (56g) butter, chilled
½ cup (120ml) ice water
⅓ pound or 5 ounces (140g) Gruyère, grated
⅓ pound or 5 ounces (140g) smoked Gouda, grated

### For the filling

1 cup (235ml) milk
2 tablespoons butter
4 shallots, peeled and sliced
4 cloves garlic, minced
1 tablespoon fresh thyme, chopped
1 tablespoon smoked paprika
1 tablespoon nutmeg
Salt and pepper, to taste
1 cup (225ml) sour cream
1 large turnip, boiled, peeled, and cut into ¼-inch (6-mm) thick slices
1 golden potato, boiled, peeled, and cut into ¼-inch (6-mm) thick slices
1 small beet, boiled, peeled, and cut into ¼-inch (6-mm) thick slices
1 pie crust and 1 sheet of pie dough for the lid
⅓ pound or 5 ounces (140g) Gruyère, grated
⅓ pound or 5 ounces (140g) smoked Gouda, grated

1 To make the crust, combine the flour and salt in a large mixing bowl. Cut the butter into small pieces and add to the flour. Using your fingers, press the butter into the flour until it reaches a crumbly texture. Add the ice water, a little at a time, until the dough binds and can be formed into a ball. Wrap in plastic wrap and refrigerate for at least 2 hours.

2 Preheat the oven to 375°F (190°C). Roll the dough out to fit a 9-inch (23 cm) pie pan. Place the crust in the pan and carefully and evenly press the dough into its bottom and sides. Trim any excess dough and set aside. Sprinkle a little of both cheeses into the crust to just cover the base.

3 To make the filling, add the milk, butter, shallots, garlic, thyme, paprika, nutmeg, and salt and pepper to a small pan. Simmer until the shallots soften. Remove the milk and shallot mixture from the heat and stir in the sour cream.

4 Cover the cheesy crust with a layer of beets. Spoon some of the creamy shallot sauce over the beets and top with another layer of cheese. On top of the cheese, add a layer of potatoes. Cover the potatoes with a layer of creamy shallot sauce and then more cheese. Add a layer of turnips on top of the potato/sauce/cheese layers and cover with more shallot sauce and cheese.

5 Roll out the remaining dough and cover the pie filling. Press down on the edges to seal, then trim the excess dough.

6 Cut slits in the center of the pie as vents. Bake in the oven for 20 minutes, or until the pie crust is golden and flaky.

# GAGH

Klingons: they're fearless warriors but they eat some nasty foods by human standards. Gagh is a popular Klingon dish composed of serpent worms. It is mentioned in *TNG*, *DS9*, and *ENT*. One of my favorite episodes of *TNG* is "A Matter of Honor," in which Riker participates in an officer exchange program and becomes acting commander of a Klingon vessel. A man after my own heart, Riker samples some Klingon cuisine in order to prepare himself for this monumental responsibility, including what looks like a giant octopus, something called Pipius Claw, and, of course, Gagh. Later in the episode, while eating dinner with the members of his Klingon crew, Riker is pressured to eat Gagh how it is supposed to be eaten: alive and wriggling. After being teased a little by the Klingon crew members, Riker eats the Gagh without flinching, which impresses the Klingons. Riker himself is impressed that Klingons are actually capable of humor, having only had Lieutenant Worf as an example of Klingon behavior. Basically, everyone learns more about each other and much bonding ensues. Definitely in my top ten *TNG* episodes.

Gagh comes in different varieties and looks a little different each time it is depicted. I tried to emulate the version from "A Matter of Honor" with some delicious stir-fried noodles. The best part about making this dish is watching as the "worms" squirm when you cook them. That may sound kinda gross, but I assure you, they are delicious. Still, if Klingon food is too strong for you...

## SERVES 2–4

4 cloves garlic, minced
6 green onions, finely chopped
10 thin slices bacon
4 medium mushrooms, thinly sliced
1 cup (70g) shredded cabbage
1 bouillon cube
3 cups (750ml) water

4–6 tablespoons soy sauce
Hot sauce (I used sriracha), to taste
8 ounces (225g) udon noodles
5 ounces (140g) regular or dried spinach fettuccine noodles
4–5 drops red food coloring (optional)
Lemon juice, to taste

1 On medium-high heat, sauté the garlic, onions, and bacon in a large, deep pan for a couple of minutes. Add the mushrooms and cabbage and sauté for a couple more minutes, combining everything.

2 Crumble in the bouillon cube, pour in the water, and let everything simmer for 5 minutes.

3 Add the soy and hot sauces and cook, stirring, for about a minute.

4 Stir in the udon and fettuccine noodles so that they separate and mix in with the other ingredients.

5 Add a few drops of red food coloring, if you like, and stir to spread evenly.

6 Cook until most of the liquid is absorbed and the noodles are soft.

7 When serving, squeeze a bit of lemon juice over the noodles.

# CAKES and CUPCAKES

A Song of Ice and Fire: **LEMON CAKES**

Portal: **DELICIOUS MOIST CAKE**

Silent Hill: **BUTTER CAKES**

Bioshock: **CREME-FILLED CAKES**

The Elder Scrolls: **SWEET ROLL**

Harry Potter: **CAULDRON CAKES**

Minecraft: **CAKE BLOCK**

Super Mario Bros.: **1UP MUSHROOM CUPCAKES**

Star Trek: **CELLULAR PEPTIDE CAKE WITH MINT FROSTING**

# LEMON CAKES

Oh, the food of *A Song of Ice and Fire*. For someone who claims not to be a great cook, George R. R. Martin sure knows how to make up some mouthwatering foodstuffs. There is an infinite amount of foods to choose from in *ASoIaF*, enough to fill an entire cookbook of its own. Happily, there is one! *A Feast of Ice and Fire* would look pretty good next to this cookbook on your nerdy cookbook shelf. It's definitely on mine! As great as the official cookbook is, I had to try my hand at a few recipes myself.

One of the more memorable sweet treats in *ASoIaF* is Sansa Stark's favorite pastry: Lemon Cakes. Lemon Cakes are mentioned fairly often in the books, but not described in detail. My impression of them is that they are a sort of teatime treat for young lords and ladies to enjoy. I pictured them being rustic in appearance (by modern standards; they'd be fancy in Elizabethan times and by Westerosi standards) and having a dense, moist texture with intense lemon flavor. My cakes are just that, and baked with a candied lemon slice for garnish.

## MAKES 20 CAKES

2 lemons, thinly sliced and seeded
1 cup (240ml) water
2½ cups (500g) granulated sugar, divided
Butter, or non-stick spray, for greasing
2½ cups (280g) flour
½ teaspoon baking powder
½ teaspoon baking soda
1 teaspoon salt
1 cup (225g) butter, softened
2 eggs
2 tablespoons lemon zest
¾ cup (175ml) fresh lemon juice, divided
1 cup (240g) buttermilk

1 Preheat the oven to 350°F (180°C) and grease a muffin tin.
2 Boil the lemon slices for about 15 minutes in the water and 1 cup (200g) of the sugar. Drain and set aside.
3 In a mixing bowl, combine the flour, baking powder, baking soda, and salt.
4 In another bowl, beat the butter and 1 cup (200g) of sugar until light and fluffy. Beat in the eggs, then stir in the lemon zest and 2 tablespoons of the lemon juice.
5 Beat in the flour mixture and then the buttermilk.
6 Place 1 lemon slice in the bottom of each muffin cup and pour the batter over the slices, dividing the batter evenly among the cups.
7 Bake until the cakes are firm and golden, about 15–20 minutes. Remove from the oven and let cool.

8  Mix together the remaining lemon juice and sugar. Poke holes into the cakes, then slowly pour the lemon and sugar mixture over the cakes so the juice is absorbed into the cakes. Set aside for 5–10 minutes.

9  Remove the cakes from the tray and serve lemon-slice side up!

# INSPIRED BY PORTAL
# DELICIOUS MOIST CAKE

I fell in love with *Portal* a little late. I remember a friend telling me about it—something about shooting portals at walls? I didn't really get it. When I finally gave the game a shot a few years later, I spent the whole night playing through and finished it in the wee hours of the morning, and then promptly passed out. In *Portal*, you find yourself in a research facility with no idea how you got there. You are told by GLaDOS (an artificial intelligence with some emotional issues) that if you complete a series of tests, you will be given cake and grief counseling. Soon you find out that the cake is a lie.

So, the cake. The infamous, ever-popular, and often-referenced cake. There is an Easter egg in the game itself where you can find a recipe for cake written in binary code, but the recipe is only an ingredients list for plain chocolate cake and lacks instructions...though it does have some great suggestions for garnishes. According to the developers, the design of the cake (which you do finally see at the end in most versions of the game) was inspired by a real cake from the Chinese bakery near their place of work, identified as a Black Forest cake. Black Forest cake is a kind of German cake that has chocolate, whipped cream, cherries, and a cherry-flavored liquor called kirschwasser. It has four layers and is filled with boozy chocolate cherry goodness. Bake this cake and throw a big party that all your friends are invited to! Don't forget to invite your weighted companion cube... Oh, wait...

## SERVES 8–10

### For the cake
Butter or nonstick spray, for greasing
1⅔ cups (160g) flour
1 cup (125g) unsweetened cocoa powder
1½ teaspoons baking soda
1 teaspoon salt
½ cup (100g) shortening
1½ cups (300g) sugar
2 eggs
1 teaspoon vanilla extract
1½ cups (360g) buttermilk
½ cup (120ml) kirsch (cherry liqueur)

### For the filling
¼ cup (60ml) kirsch
2 × 14.5-ounce (411g) can tart cherries
3 cups (700ml) heavy whipping cream
¼ cup (25g) confectioners' sugar
3 tablespoons cocoa powder

### For the garnish
1 semisweet chocolate bar, frozen
8 maraschino cherries, stems removed
1 white candle

1 Preheat the oven to 350°F (180°C) and grease and flour two 8-inch (20 cm) cake pans, or line with parchment paper.

2 Combine the flour, cocoa, baking soda, and the salt in a large mixing bowl. Set aside.

3 Beat the shortening and sugar together until fluffy. Add the eggs and vanilla and beat thoroughly.

4 Slowly beat the flour mixture into the sugar mixture, occasionally alternating with the buttermilk. Beat until everything is combined.

5 Pour the batter into the cake pans and bake for 35–40 minutes, or until a wooden pick comes out clean when inserted into the center of the cakes. Let the cakes cool completely—by keeping them in the fridge for a few hours, they will be easier to cut.

6 Meanwhile, make the filling. Drain the canned cherries in a colander to remove most of the juice.

7 Beat the whipping cream with the confectioners' sugar until it thickens to the desired texture.

8 Set aside a small amount of the whipped cream mixture for decorating the cake. Mix the cocoa powder into the remaining whipped cream mixture.

9 After the cakes have cooled, cut each cake in half horizontally to make four layers. Sprinkle each layer with the ½ cup (120ml) of kirsch.

10 Place one cake layer on the serving dish you wish to use. Spread about one-sixth of the whipped cream on the layer and one-third of the cherries on top of the whipped cream.

11 Place the second cake layer on top of the first. Spread one-sixth of the whipped cream on the second layer and one-third of the cherries on top.

12 Add the third cake layer. Spread one-sixth of the whipped cream on top along with the remaining cherries.

13 Top with the last cake layer. Frost the top and sides of the cake with the remaining whipped cream frosting.

14 Use a vegetable peeler to create thin shavings from the chocolate bar. Gently pat the shavings onto the sides and top of the cake, completely coating it. Use gloves—melting chocolate can get messy!

15 Use the reserved whipped cream frosting to dot eight small circles around the top of the cake. Place your non-stemmed maraschino cherries on each one.

16 Place a white candle in the center of the cake and light it. Congratulations, you have made the cake a reality!

# BUTTER CAKES

I am a huge fan of *Silent Hill* and have long lamented that it's not exactly a great environment for noms. Being trapped in a terrifying hell dimension of guilt and torture doesn't exactly make you hungry, as Heather points out in *Silent Hill 3*. So, when I discovered the presence of the mysterious Butter Cakes, I was ecstatic. Apparently, there's a running gag among *Silent Hill* fans to try to find all the boxes. So far, Butter Cakes have been discovered in the second, third, and fourth games, which just so happen to be my favorites in the series. I know that not a lot of people like *SH4*, but personally, I think it has the scariest monster in any game ever—the one with the baby heads that points and whispers at you. Eeeeeeesh.

## MAKES 12 CAKES

### For the cakes

Butter or nonstick spray,
   for greasing
½ cup or 1 stick (112g)
   unsalted butter, softened
1 cup (200g) sugar
2 eggs, divided
1 teaspoon vanilla extract
1⅓ cups (180g) cake flour
Pinch of salt
2 teaspoons baking powder
¼ cup (60ml) whole milk
1 tablespoon imitation
   butter flavor
Pinch of salt

### For the topping

¼ cup or ½ stick (55g) butter
1 cup (100g) confectioners'
   sugar
1 teaspoon imitation butter
   flavor
1 tablespoon milk
12 maraschino cherries

1 Preheat the oven to 350°F (180°C). Grease or line a muffin tin with cupcake liners.

2 In a large mixing bowl, use a mixer to cream together the butter and sugar for the cakes. Add one egg and continue mixing. Once the egg is incorporated, add the other egg and the vanilla extract and continue to mix for a minute or so until smooth.

3 In a separate bowl, combine the flour, salt, and baking powder.

4 Slowly mix the dry ingredients in with the creamed butter and sugar mixture. Finally, slowly mix in the milk until batter is smooth. Divide batter evenly among the muffin tin cups.

5 Bake between 20–25 minutes, or until edges of cakes are golden and a toothpick inserted into the cakes comes out clean.

6 Around 15 minutes before the cupcakes finish baking, make the glaze. Heat the butter in a saucepan over medium heat until golden brown, about 10 minutes.

7 Pour butter into a bowl. Add the confectioners' sugar, imitation butter flavor, and milk, and stir until smooth. If glaze is too thick, add more milk; too thin, add more sugar.

8 While cakes are still hot, pour the glaze on top of them and insert one cherry into the center of each cake by pressing down gently so it's partially imbedded.

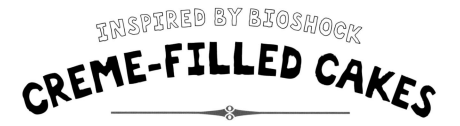

# INSPIRED BY BIOSHOCK
# CREME-FILLED CAKES

I lack hand-eye coordination so I tend to be very bad at shooters, and because of that, it's hard for me to get into them. *Bioshock* is an exception. Developed by Irrational Games, *Bioshock* is almost universally acknowledged as an exceptional and unforgettable gaming experience. It takes place in a secret underwater city called Rapture. Rapture was built by an ambitious American shortly after the end of World War II for the purpose of forming a completely isolated capitalist society untainted by government or religion. Shockingly, this didn't exactly work out. The isolation of Rapture made it somewhat of a time capsule, but the lack of moral or governmental limitations in invention has allowed for some very advanced technology to be created, so it's a completely unique game environment.

The food is mostly of a pre-packaged variety with a focus on convenience. These Creme-Filled Cakes are one of only three kinds of food found in the game, along with potato chips and Pep Bars. There is more than twice that amount of alcohol varieties in the game, which tells you a lot about the citizens of Rapture. The cakes come in a sort of log shape, much like a certain beloved snack cake found in the real world. They also appear to be filled with chocolate creme and have sort of a squiggly frosting design on top.

## MAKES 8–12 CAKES

### For the cakes

2 cups (250g) cake flour
1¼ cups (250g) sugar
1 tablespoon baking powder
1 teaspoon salt
½ cup or 1 stick (112g) butter, softened
1 cup (235ml) milk
1 teaspoon vanilla extract
2 eggs
Nonstick spray, for greasing
1 tube of ready-made white decorative frosting

### For the chocolate creme filling

1 jar or 7 ounces (200g) marshmallow creme
⅓ cup (40g) confectioners' sugar
½ cup (60g) cocoa powder
½ cup (100g) shortening
1 teaspoon vanilla extract
1 tablespoon evaporated milk
Pinch of salt

*cont.*

1 Preheat oven to 350°F (180°C).

2 If you don't have a canoe pan, I recommend making the cake molds first. Tear out a 12-inch- (30 cm) long sheet of aluminum foil. Fold it once lengthwise and then once crosswise. Place a spice jar in the center and wrap the aluminum foil around it, tucking in the ends to create a trough-like shape. Make sure the tops are open so you can pour in your batter. Remove the spice jar. Repeat until you have about 10 of these.

3 In a large mixing bowl, sift together the flour, sugar, baking powder, and salt.

4 Add the butter, milk, and vanilla and beat with a hand mixer for 3–4 minutes. Add the eggs and beat for 3 more minutes.

5 Spray the cake mold(s) with nonstick spray. Pour the batter evenly among the cups—they should be around three-quarters full. Depending on the size of the spice jar used, you can end up with anywhere between 8 and 12 cakes.

6 Bake the cakes for about 30 minutes, or until a toothpick inserted in the center comes out clean. Let the cakes cool in their cases, then remove and transfer to a wire rack to cool completely.

7 Meanwhile, make the filling. Put all the filling ingredients into a mixing bowl and beat until light and fluffy.

8 Place the filling into a pastry bag with a narrow attachment. Using a chopstick, evenly poke three holes into the bottom of one of the cakes. Sort of swish your chopstick around a bit in there to create more room for the filling. Pipe the chocolate filling into each of the holes, repeating this process for each cake.

9 When all the cakes are filled, attach a narrow frosting piper onto the tube of white decorative frosting and draw squiggles on the top of each of the cakes.

10 Stuff all the cakes into your mouth immediately while in the middle of a battle.

# SWEET ROLL

The highly desirable Sweet Roll is probably the most well-known food from *The Elder Scrolls* series. The stolen Sweet Roll has been a running gag in *Elder Scroll* games dating all the way back to *Arena*, where it was referenced in a theoretical question to determine your character class based on the morality of your answer. Now, Sweet Rolls are an alchemy ingredient in *Oblivion*, an actual consumable item in *Skyrim*, and even appeared in *Fallout*.

It is unknown what exactly a Sweet Roll is; what is known is that they are so tasty that people want to steal them from you—a crime punishable by a night in jail. Presumably, they are a delicious sugary baked good. In *Oblivion*, they have a shape sort of like a tall muffin or a chef's hat. In *Skyrim*, they look like a volcano with white icing. The difference in appearance may be due to regional differences in Tamriel, as *Oblivion* takes place in Cyrodill and *Skyrim* takes place in…Skyrim. I went with the *Skyrim* appearance. Enjoy a volcano-shaped cinnamon cake filled with sugary, buttery, nutty goodness, topped with cream-cheese icing. There are two ways to bake these: with a mini Bundt-cake pan for a perfect shape (these can be found fairly easily online) or in a standard glass measuring cup.

## MAKES 2–6 ROLLS

### For the cake

1½ cups (180g) flour
½ cup (100g) granulated sugar
2 teaspoons baking powder
Pinch of salt
2 tablespoons ground
 cinnamon
⅓ (80ml) cup milk
1 egg
2 teaspoons vanilla extract
¼ cup or ½ stick (55g) butter,
 melted
Butter or nonstick spray,
 for greasing

### For the filling

¼ cup or ½ stick (55g)
 butter, softened
½ cup (30g) chopped pecan
 nuts
1 tablespoon ground
 cinnamon
¼ cup (60g) packed brown
 sugar

### For the icing

¼ cup or 2 ounces (60g)
 cream cheese, softened
1½ cups (150g)
 confectioners' sugar
2 tablespoons milk

1 Preheat the oven to 350°F (180°C).

2 To make the cake, combine the flour, sugar, baking powder, salt, and cinnamon in a large mixing bowl.

3 Mix together the milk, egg, vanilla extract, and butter in a separate bowl.

4 Add the wet ingredients to the dry ingredients and combine thoroughly.

5 Grease the inside of an oven-safe glass measuring cup or mini Bundt-cake pan. If using a glass cup, add the batter to the 1 or 1½ cup (240 or 350ml) line, depending on how tall you want the cake to be. If using the Bundt-cake pan, simply add an even amount of batter to each cup.

6 Bake for 25–30 minutes, or until you can stick in a knife and it comes out clean.

7 Remove from the oven and let the cake(s) cool. Once cool, carefully remove from the measuring cup or pan so it does not break.

8 If using a glass measuring cup, the cake is going to be upside down (so the wider part is at the bottom) and may be awkwardly rounded on the bottom side. To fix this, simply cut off the rounded bottom with a knife to make it level. Set the cake down with the wider leveled side on the bottom. Use a spoon or fork to carve a hole at the top of the cake—this is where you will put the filling.

9 To make the filling, mix together all of the ingredients. Stuff the mixture into the hole(s) in the cake(s).

10 For the icing, whisk or beat together all of the ingredients until smooth and thick. Gently drizzle the icing on top of the cake(s).

11 Serve or have the Sweet Rolls all to yourself! Remember, in *Skyrim*, stealing a Sweet Roll is punishable by a night in jail.

# CAULDRON CAKES

Cauldron Cakes are one of the many magical treats that witches and wizards enjoy in the world of *Harry Potter*. They are purchased by an eleven-year-old Harry Potter for himself and his new friend, Ron, on their very first journey to Hogwarts on the Hogwarts Express. J. K. Rowling doesn't really explain how the cakes look or taste in the books, so readers have come up with some imaginative interpretations. For this recipe, I was inspired by the artwork on J. K. Rowling's website, Pottermore, in which they look like cute little chocolate cakes filled with some sort of green goo to resemble a bubbling cauldron. Sidenote: If you are a fan of *Harry Potter*, own a computer, and have suffered *Potter* withdrawal since the books and movies ended, get thee to Pottermore right now. Not only is it an extremely fun way to relive the books, but there's just a ton of wonderful art, games, and extra information to be gleaned from Rowling herself. Yes, I am absolutely on Pottermore, and will definitely be your friend. My name is ScarletHolly25290 and I'm in Ravenclaw. Add me! No, I will not duel you. I don't believe in violence. Okay, that's not really why I won't duel you…I'm just really bad at dueling.

## MAKES 20 CAKES

### For the cake

Butter or nonstick spray, for greasing
1 cup (120g) flour
⅓ cup (40g) unsweetened cocoa powder
1 teaspoon baking powder
1 teaspoon allspice
½ teaspoon salt
½ cup (100g) shortening
¾ cup (150g) sugar
1 egg
1 teaspoon vanilla extract
1 cup (240g) buttermilk

### For the topping

1 tablespoon cornstarch
½ tablespoon water
14-ounce (396g) can sweetened condensed milk
¼ cup (50g) shortening
A few drops of green food coloring
Flavor extract (your choice)
Pearl sprinkles
Green sugar sprinkles

1 Preheat the oven to 350°F (180°C) and grease a muffin tin.

2 In a large mixing bowl, combine the flour, cocoa powder, baking powder, allspice, and salt.

3 In a separate, smaller mixing bowl, beat together the shortening and sugar. Add the egg and vanilla and beat until fluffy.

4 Slowly beat in the flour mixture, occasionally alternating with the buttermilk.

5 Evenly divide the batter among the holes in the muffin tin(s).

6 Bake for about 20 minutes, or until a fork inserted into the cakes comes out clean.

7 Let the cakes cool, then remove them from the tin and transfer to a wire rack to cool completely.

8 Meanwhile, make the topping. Combine the cornstarch and water to form a paste.

9 Beat together all the remaining topping ingredients—except the sprinkles—including the cornstarch paste you just made. The finished texture should be like a thick and gooey slime. If it's too runny, add more shortening; if it's too thick (like frosting), add more sweetened condensed milk.

10 Take the cooled cakes and carve out a shallow hole on the bottom side of each one to be the inside of the cauldron that holds the goo.

11 Spoon the goo into the holes so that they are almost overflowing, then top with sprinkles.

12 Accio Cauldron Cakes!

# INSPIRED BY MINECRAFT
## CAKE BLOCK

*Minecraft* is an award-winning indie game that has reached an unfathomable level of popularity in a relatively short amount of time. In the game, you mine and craft materials in order to build yourself a shelter and survive, or you run around punching things and get beaten to death by zombies and/or die of starvation—like me. One of the best things about *Minecraft* is that you are given absolute freedom to build whatever you want, however you want. This freedom has allowed players to make some very elaborate worlds and buildings, especially in the game's creative mode. Everything in the game—from the animals to the clouds—is rendered as textured blocks, including the cake.

Most of the prepared food in *Minecraft* is only shown in your inventory, but the cake is an exception. The cake block is made by combining three buckets of milk, two units of sugar, three units of wheat, and one egg. When the cake is crafted, it needs to be placed on top of another block in order to be enjoyed. Each slice of cake recovers two hunger units, and eating the entire cake will recover twelve hunger units. Unlike the other foods in *Minecraft*, slices of cake are eaten instantaneously and you can gobble down the whole cake in seconds—much like real life. The cake is depicted as having white icing and little red pixels on top.

This recipe is for my favorite white cake layered with strawberry jam filling to complement the red pixels. You will need to use fondant to recreate the geometric patterns and clean lines of the cake's topping.

### SERVES 6–10

1 cup or 2 sticks (225g) butter, softened
2 cups (450g) white sugar
4 eggs
1 tablespoon vanilla extract
3 cups (360g) cake flour
1 tablespoon baking powder
¾ cup (175ml) whole milk

1 teaspoon salt
Butter or nonstick spray, for greasing
1½ cups (485g) strawberry jelly
White fondant
Red fondant (recommended) or red food dye

*cont.*

1. Preheat the oven to 350°F (180°C).

2. Cream together the butter and sugar then add the eggs and vanilla extract and continue mixing.

3. Mix in the flour, baking powder, and salt.

4. Grease the baking pans and divide the batter equally between them. Bake for 30–40 minutes, or until a fork inserted into the center of each cake comes out clean. Remove from the oven and leave to cool.

5. Once cool, carefully level the tops of the cakes using a sharp knife.

6. Set one cake on a board and spoon half of the jelly on top, spreading it around evenly, keeping it about 1 inch (2.5 cm) in from the outer edges of the cake.

7. Set the other cake on top and spread the rest of the jelly over the top and slightly over the edge of the second cake layer.

8. Here comes the hard part: fondant is unforgiving and difficult to work with, but I'll do my best to explain this next step. Roll out the white fondant until you have a surface area large enough to cover your entire cake.

9. Carefully lift the fondant sheet by gently flipping one end over the rolling pin and raising it up and onto the top of the cake, making sure it is completely covered. Then, using your hands, gently press the fondant around the cake, trying to avoid making any folds or creases.

10. Using a sharp knife, scalpel, or scissors, cut out the square pattern in the fondant on the sides of the cake. I highly recommend creating a template or stencil by cutting the shape out of some cardboard before attempting this, and using a photo for reference.

11. You have a few options for the red squares on the top of the cake. Option 1: Roll out some pre-made red fondant and cut out the square shapes. Wet them lightly on the back and arrange them on top of the cake. This is the easiest and best-looking option. Option 2: Roll out the white fondant, cut out the square shapes, and paint them individually with red food dye. Then lightly wet the back (unpainted) side of each and carefully arrange them on top of the cake. Option 3: Position the white fondant squares and paint them in situ with red food dye.

12. Cut the cake into six (or more) square slices and enjoy!

# INSPIRED BY SUPER MARIO BROS.
# 1UP MUSHROOM CUPCAKES

Like most people born after 1985, I grew up playing *Super Mario Bros.* games. The series, created by Nintendo's very own mad genius Shigeru Miyamoto, is one of the most widely known and beloved game series of all time. The games feature Mario, a portly Italian plumber with inexplicably superior athletic ability and stamina. He is in love with Princess Toadstool, aka Peach. Unfortunately for Mario, the princess is kidnapped by King Koopa, aka Bowser, about every year or so. Fun fact: Mario actually made his first appearance as Jumpman in Nintendo's 1981 arcade game *Donkey Kong*.

One of the many iconic items in the Mario series is the 1Up Mushroom. Unlike the red toadstool, which allows Mario to grow in size, the 1Up Mushroom gives Mario another life and another chance to fall into the abyss or be killed by fire-breathing plants. The 1Up's appearance has changed over the years, but most will recognize it as the bright green toadstool with white spots. I generally try to avoid making cakes that look like things that are not supposed to be cakes, but this is an exception. Mario was the catalyst that made gaming what it is today and is a piece of geek cultural history. Short of encouraging people to eat a raw toadstool (do NOT eat raw toadstools...) there wasn't any other way to pay tribute to Mario in food.

You can make the frosting in this one either green or red, depending on whether you want another life or to grow in size. Well, eat too many of these babies and you'll grow in size either way.

*cont.*

## MAKES 12 CUPCAKES

### For the cakes

Butter or nonstick spray,
    for greasing
½ cup or 1 stick (112g)
    butter, softened
1 cup (225g) sugar
2 eggs, divided
1 teaspoon vanilla extract
1⅓ cups (180g) cake flour
Pinch of salt
1 teaspoon baking powder
¼ cup (60ml) whole milk

### For the frosting/topping

½ cup or 1 stick (112g)
    butter, softened
½ cup (112g) shortening
2 cups (250g) powdered
    sugar
½ tablespoon milk
Green or red food dye
2 teaspoons imitation butter
    flavoring
White chocolate buttons or
    white modeling chocolate
    or white fondant

1 Preheat the oven to 350°F (180°C) and grease or line a muffin tin with cupcake liners.

2 In a large mixing bowl, cream together the butter and sugar for the cakes.

3 Add one of the eggs and continue mixing. Once the first egg is fully incorporated, add the other egg and the vanilla extract and continue to mix for a minute or so until smooth.

4 In a separate bowl, sift together the flour, salt, and baking powder.

5 Slowly mix the dry ingredients into the creamed butter and sugar mixture, then slowly mix in the milk until the batter is smooth.

6 Divide the batter evenly among the muffin-tin cups until each is three-quarters full.

7 Bake for 20–25 minutes, or until the edges of the cakes are golden and a toothpick inserted in the center comes out clean.

8 Make the frosting by first creaming together the butter and shortening.

9 Whip the powdered sugar into the butter and shortening, then add the milk, green or red food dye, and imitation butter flavor, and continue to whip until you get the right consistency and color. The frosting should be spreadable but stiff; if it's too runny add more powdered sugar, if it's too stiff add more milk.

10 Spread the green or red frosting on top of the cupcakes and decorate with white dots.

# CELLULAR PEPTIDE CAKE WITH MINT FROSTING

This is from my very favorite *TNG* episode, "Phastasms," in which the android Data is testing a new program that allows him to dream. It turns out that androids do not dream of electric sheep; they dream of rotary telephones in their belly, brain slurpees, and their colleagues being turned into cakes.

The cake, which is human shaped and has Deanna Troi's head, is described by an uncharacteristically excited Worf as a "cellular peptide cake with mint frosting." Cellular peptide isn't actually a thing, but it is described in the episode as a chain of molecules found in living things. This recipe is for a moist white cake with some very blue, mint-flavored frosting. I used yogurt as a moistener for the cake itself because yogurt contains living bacteria and represents the cellular peptide. It's important to make the cake look like a *TNG* Starfleet Medical uniform, which is much easier than it sounds. Enjoy this lovely cake with a brain slurpee to wash it down! Mmm…delicious.

## SERVES 4–6

### For the cake

Butter or nonstick spray,
  for greasing
2¾ cups (320g) flour
1 ⅔ cups (320g) sugar
1 tablespoon baking powder
¾ teaspoon salt
¾ cup or 1½ sticks (170g)
  unsalted butter, softened
4 egg whites
1 egg
1 cup (245g) vanilla yogurt
2 teaspoons vanilla extract

### For the frosting

1½ cups confectioners'
  sugar
2 tablespoons milk
1 tablespoon shortening
½ teaspoon vanilla extract
½ teaspoon mint or
  peppermint extract,
  or to taste
Blue food coloring
Black food coloring

1 Preheat the oven to 350°F (180°C) and grease a 9 × 9-inch (23 × 23 cm) baking pan.

2 Combine the flour, sugar, baking powder, and salt in a large mixing bowl.

3 Add the softened butter and mix until crumbly. Add the egg whites, followed by the whole egg, and beat well.

4 In a separate bowl, whisk together the yogurt with the vanilla extract. Add this mixture to the batter and beat until fluffy.

5 Pour the batter into the baking pan and bake for 30–40 minutes, or until a knife or toothpick inserted into the center comes out clean. Let the cake cool and set in the pan.

6 While it sets, prepare the frosting. Combine all the frosting ingredients in a small bowl in the order listed. Beat until you reach a creamy consistency. Add more confectioners' sugar if the frosting is too thin.

7 Divide the frosting between two bowls. In one bowl, add the blue food coloring. You will need a lot to get a deep blue; in the other bowl, mix in the black food coloring. Stir until the color is evenly dispersed.

8 Remove the cooled cake from the pan and cut off part of its sides to make a "T" or torso shape.

9 Emulate a *TNG*-style blue (sciences) Starfleet uniform when frosting.

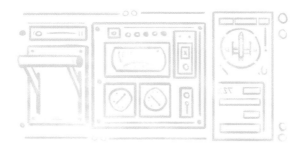

# DESSERTS

---

The Chronicles of Narnia: **TURKISH DELIGHT**

Avatar: The Last Airbender: **AIR NOMAD'S FRUIT PIES**

Harry Potter: **TREACLE TARTS**

Harry Potter: **PUMPKIN PASTIES**

Kingdom Hearts: **SEA-SALT ICE CREAM**

Pokémon: **POFFINS**

South Park: **CHOCOLATE SALTY BALLS**

# TURKISH DELIGHT

Turkish Delight isn't fictional at all, but it's such a staple of fantasy food I couldn't not make a recipe—that would pretty much be nerd blasphemy. Those who have read *The Lion, The Witch and the Wardrobe* will remember the very tense moment when little Edmund meets the sinister White Queen and stupidly reveals the location of his siblings for a bit of Turkish Delight. Edmund was kind of a jerk at that early point in the story, but the way Turkish Delight was described in the book made it seem like such a heavenly treat that you could almost—almost— empathize with the little brat.

So, Turkish Delight is actually a sweet and chewy confection that is traditionally flavored with rose water and nuts and served with a coating of confectioners' sugar. I've kept this recipe very old school because why mess with tradition when it's already so good you'll sell out your own brothers and sisters for a piece?

## MAKES 26–36 PIECES

1 cup (235ml) water
2 tablespoons gelatin
1¾ cups (150g) sugar
¼ teaspoon citric acid
½ cup (50g) pistachios, shelled and chopped
1 teaspoon vanilla extract
2 teaspoons rose water or other flavoring extract of your choice
¼ cup (25g) confectioners' sugar
2 tablespoons cornstarch
Few drops of food coloring (optional)
Oil, for greasing

1  Place the water in a large saucepan and sprinkle over the gelatin. Set aside until the gelatin is a little springy.

2  Add the sugar and citric acid to the gelatin water, place the pan over a gentle heat, and stir constantly until dissolved.

3  Bring the mixture to a boil. Boil for 15 minutes without stirring. Remove from heat and set aside for 10 minutes.

4  Stir in the vanilla extract, rose water, pistachios, and a few drops of food coloring, if using.

5  Pour into a greased 6 × 6-inch (15 × 15 cm) baking pan. Leave uncovered in a cool place for 24 hours.

6  Sift the confectioners' sugar and corn flour together onto a sheet of parchment paper. Turn out the set Turkish delight onto the paper and cut into squares using a sharp knife.

7  Toss pieces in the confectioners' sugar mixture so that all sides are coated. Pack the squares into airtight containers lined with parchment paper and dust with the remaining confectioners' sugar mixture.

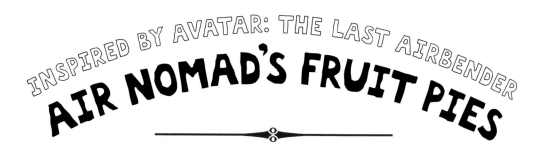

# AIR NOMAD'S FRUIT PIES

### INSPIRED BY AVATAR: THE LAST AIRBENDER

It's impossible to resist a series with so many good food moments. For some context, the people of Avatar fall into four different nations that are each devoted to one of the four elements: earth, air, fire, and water. Some people in these nations have command of their national element; this skill is known as bending. The national element and the bending skill has a lot of influence on the culture of the nation and, of course, their cuisine. The fire nation tends to like things spicy, the water tribe eats a lot of seafood and soups, etc. These Fruit Pies are an airbender dessert that appeared in the third episode of the series in a flashback/memory of Avatar Ang's, in which he fondly remembers his airbending master making the pies so that they could airbend them onto the heads of the other air monks. Ang's master tells him that the secret is in the "gooey center." In a later episode, Ang divulges that the pies are his favorite food!

My idea for this recipe was to make a delicious coconut frangipane pie tart with a gooey jelly center. It's topped with colorful lime-flavored whipped cream, which will require you to do some real airbending!

## MAKES 1 x 9-INCH (23 CM) PIE

### For the crust
1¾ cups (210g) flour, plus extra for dusting
¾ cup or 1½ sticks (170g) butter, chilled and cubed
¼ cup (50g) granulated sugar
2 egg yolks
1 tablespoon orange zest

### For the filling
½ cup or 1 stick (113g) butter, softened
½ cup (100g) granulated sugar
2 medium eggs, beaten
¾ cup (85g) almond meal
2 teaspoons coconut extract
1 teaspoon cornstarch
Pinch of salt
3 cups (240g) jelly or jam (I suggest mango, passion fruit, or pineapple flavored)

### For the topping
1 cup (240ml) heavy whipping cream
½ cup (50g) confectioners' sugar
Zest of 1 lime
Few drops of food coloring color of your choice

1 First, make the crust. Blend the flour and butter in a food processor until crumbly. Add the sugar and blend again briefly to combine.

2 Add the egg yolks and orange zest and pulse until it comes together. You may need to add a little bit of water if it seems dry.

3 Wrap the pastry in plastic wrap and chill for about 30 minutes.

4 Preheat the oven to 375°F (190°C). While oven is preheating, make the filling. Cream together the butter and sugar until smooth. Add the almond meal and blend well.

5 Add the eggs and stir until thoroughly combined, then stir in the extract, cornstarch, and salt.

6 After the dough has chilled, roll it out to fit a 9-inch (23 cm) pie pan. Place the dough in the pan and carefully and evenly press it into the bottom and sides. Trim any excess dough and discard.

7 Spoon the jelly or jam onto the bottom of the pie and spread evenly.

8 Spoon the filling on top of the jelly or jam and spread evenly, completely covering the jam.

9 Bake for 30 minutes, or until center is firm but springy to the touch. Let cool.

10 Make the whipped cream. Add all of the topping ingredients into a large mixing bowl and whip together with a mixer until peaks start to form. Be careful not to whip too much and make butter. Cover the bowl with plastic wrap and place in the refrigerator until ready to use.

11 When the pie has cooled, use a piping bag with large star attachment to pipe the whipped cream topping onto the center of the pie in a swirling motion.

12 Airbend the pie onto someone's head.

# TREACLE TARTS

Harry Potter's favorite dessert! Harry loves Treacle Tarts so much that he smells them even when in the presence of Amortentia.

Treacle Tarts are a traditional English dessert, popular among children and made with golden syrup. Golden syrup has an irresistible nutty and buttery flavor, with almost the same consistency as honey. I can see why Harry likes it. It's truly liquid gold and my new favorite thing ever. Watch out, Felix Felicis! Well, pop the stuff in a flaky tart crust and it is pure heaven. And by "heaven" I mean Hogwarts.

## MAKES 12 TARTS

### For the crusts

1¾ cups (210g) flour, plus extra for dusting
¾ cup or 1½ sticks (170g) butter, chilled and diced
¼ cup (50g) sugar
2 egg yolks
1 tablespoon orange zest

### For the filling

1 cup (350g) golden syrup
1 tablespoon molasses
2 tablespoons butter
Pinch of salt
6 tablespoons bread crumbs
3 tablespoons heavy cream
1 tablespoon flour
1 tablespoon lemon zest
1 egg, whisked

Whipped cream, clotted cream, or vanilla ice cream, to serve

1 First, make the crusts. Blend the flour and butter in a food processor until crumbly.

2 Add the sugar and blend again briefly to combine.

3 Add the egg yolks and the orange zest and pulse until it comes together. You may need to add a little bit of water if it seems dry.

4 Wrap the pastry in plastic wrap and chill for about 30 minutes.

5 Preheat the oven to 375°F (190°C).

6 Meanwhile, make the filling. Heat the golden syrup and molasses in a saucepan over medium heat for 3–5 minutes, or until loosened, stirring occasionally.

7 Remove the syrup from the heat and stir in the butter, salt, breadcrumbs, cream, flour, and zest until combined. Stir in the egg and set aside.

8 Roll out the pastry on a floured surface until it is ⅛ inch (3 mm) thick, then stamp or cut out circles big enough to fit your tart tins. You can use a cookie cutter for this if necessary.

9 Mold the circular dough cut-outs into the bottoms and sides of the tart tins, fill each with the treacle filling, and bake for approximately 20 minutes, or until the treacle is firm and set and the crust is golden.

10 Serve hot or cold, topped with whipped cream, clotted cream, or vanilla ice cream, if desired!

# PUMPKIN PASTIES

Another mouthwatering *Harry Potter* classic! Pumpkin Pasties are mentioned fairly often in the *Harry Potter* series, though never described in detail. They are sold at the Honeyduke's Trolley on the Hogwarts Express. They were one of the first wizard foods Harry Potter ever ate, along with Chocolate Frogs and Cauldron Cakes.

A pasty is a sort of hand pie, thought to have originated in Cornwall, England, where they are the regional specialty. They are semi-circular in shape and are traditionally made with pie crust filled with meat, potatoes, and other savories. However, because in *Harry Potter* Pumpkin Pasties are sold alongside other sweets, there is a consensus that they are a dessert. I've made a simple pastry crust filled with spiced, sweetened, gooey pumpkin goodness. It's sort of like a delicious, portable pocket of pumpkin pie!

## MAKES 12 PASTIES

### For the crust

3½ cups (420g) flour
Pinch of salt
5 teaspoons sugar
¾ cup or 1½ sticks (170g) butter, cubed
½ cup (100g) shortening
1 cup ice water, divided

### For the filling

2 eggs, whisked
1 cup (100g) sugar
15-ounce (425g) can pumpkin
2 tablespoons unsalted butter, melted, plus extra for the pasty crusts
½ teaspoon salt
2 teaspoons ground cinnamon, plus extra for the pasty crusts
1 teaspoon ground ginger
1 teaspoon ground cloves
1 teaspoon ground cardamon
1 teaspoon allspice
12-ounce (354ml) can evaporated milk

1 First, make the crust. Combine the flour, salt, and sugar until well blended. Add the butter cubes and toss until coated. Using your hands, rub the butter into the flour until dough is in bean-size pieces.

2 Add the shortening to the dough and toss, then rub the shortening into the flour using the same method as with the butter, until you have pea-size pieces.

3 Sprinkle in about half of the ice water and use your hands to squeeze the dough together, being careful not to overwork it. Keep adding a little bit of ice water at a time until the dough comes together but is not wet—you may not need to use all of the water.

4 Form the dough into a ball, cover with plastic wrap, and put in the fridge for at least 30 minutes.

5 Meanwhile, make the filling. Add the eggs and sugar to a mixing bowl and combine until well blended.

6 Stir in the pumpkin, butter, salt, and spices. Pour in the evaporated milk and stir well.

7 In a large greased casserole dish, bake the filling at 425°F (220°C) for 15 minutes. Reduce the oven temperature to 350°F (180°C) and continue baking for 45 minutes, or until your fork comes out clean when inserted into the filling. Let it cool completely.

8 Roll out the pastry until thin and cut into circles about 4 inches (10cm) in diameter.

9 Put a heaping spoonful of the pumpkin mixture toward one side of the center of the circle. Fold over the crust into a half-circle and firmly press the edges closed.

10 Cut three small slits in the top for venting and place on a greased cookie sheet.

11 Raise the oven temperature to 400°F (200°C) and bake until crust is a light golden brown, around 10 minutes.

12 If desired, mix some cinnamon and melted butter together and brush the pasties after they come out of the oven.

# SEA-SALT ICE CREAM

## INSPIRED BY KINGDOM HEARTS

*Kingdom Hearts* is where *Final Fantasy* and Disney collide. In the first game, you play as Sora, a kid from an isolated island who finds himself thrown into a crazy adventure involving Disney and *Final Fantasy* characters alike. In the beginning of the second game, however, you are another kid, named Roxas. Roxas and his friends live in a place called Twilight Town and spend their time getting into trouble and eating Sea-Salt Ice Cream on top of the clock tower overlooking the town. Later in the game, the characters of *Kingdom Hearts II* can often be seen talking about—and eating—this delicious salty-sweet dessert.

Apparently, *Kingdom Hearts II* director Tetsuya Nomura had this ice cream on a trip to the Tokyo Disneyland Resort and liked it so much, he decided to work with Disney to put it into the games. It has a characteristic sky-blue color and is only ever seen being eaten on a popsicle stick. I have learned a lot since I originally posted the recipe for Sea-Salt Ice Cream on my blog, so I have revised the original recipe and I think it is greatly improved. The ice cream is sweet, cold, smooth, and creamy with a hint of sea salt to finish. Enjoy this with your best buddies at twilight on a warm summer day.

## MAKES 4 PINTS

5 cups (600ml) heavy cream
2½ cups (570ml) whole milk
1 teaspoon vanilla extract
1½ cups (300g) sugar, divided
Sea salt, to taste
12 large egg yolks
Blue food coloring
Nonstick spray (optional)

1 Simmer the cream, milk, vanilla extract, and 1 cup (200g) of the sugar in a large pot, stirring with a wooden spoon, for about 15 minutes.

2 Stir the sea salt into the cream mixture in extremely tiny amounts and taste as you go. Keep adding until you get a subtle salty aftertaste.

3 Combine the egg yolks in a large mixing bowl and lightly whisk them. Slowly add the remaining ½ cup (100g) of sugar and continue to whisk until the sugar is completely dissolved and the eggs are thick and pale yellow.

4 Gradually whisk in about 4 cups (950ml) of the hot cream mixture.

5 Once the hot cream is evenly whisked into the egg yolks, pour it all back into the saucepan with the rest of the cream. Turn the heat to medium-low.

6 Add a few drops of the blue food coloring, a little at a time, and stir constantly until the color is right and the custard thickens, about 12 minutes. Make sure not to boil the custard.

7 Chill the ice-cream base in the refrigerator until cold.

8 If using an ice-cream maker, transfer the chilled ice-cream base to your machine and churn according to the manufacturer's instructions—it should come out like soft-serve. Spoon into a freezer-proof container and place in the freezer until ready to serve.

9 If not using an ice-cream maker, place chilled ice cream in a frozen stainless-steel mixing bowl and let the mixture sit until the edges start to freeze, about 15–20 minutes. Use a spatula or whisk to rapidly stir the ice cream, mixing in the frozen edges. Return the stainless-steel bowl to the freezer. Vigorously stir the ice cream every 30 minutes until it is firm, between 4–6 times. If it's too hard to stir, place in the fridge until it softens, then stir again.

10 If you're making popsicles, spray the insides of the molds with nonstick cooking spray and pour the ice cream into each mold. Add the sticks and freeze for at least four hours.

# POFFINS

Pokémon is a worldwide phenomenon. The video games and anime TV series blew up in a big way in the '90s and the brand has, ahem, evolved over time. Now there are movies, card games, collectibles, and even knockoffs based on the beloved Japanese animal things. Amazingly, the brand is just as popular today as it was over a decade ago, if not even more so. On planet Earth today, approximately zero humans are unaware of the existence of Pikachu. I'm old enough to remember the world before Pokémon and let me tell you, it was about 25 percent less adorable.

As most know, the basic premise of Pokémon is that there are these creatures and you must collect them all *because reasons*. Well, sometimes your Pokémon need to eat. One of the more interesting consumables, Poffins, are depicted as little multicolored football-shaped pastries. When a Pokémon eats a Poffin, one of their conditions (smart, cute, tough, etc.) improves based on what kind of berry is used in the creation of the Poffin. I tried a few different things for poffins, including filling them with jelly and trying to incorporate fruit in the dough itself, but let's just say it wasn't very effective. See what I did there? Their final incarnation, which I have included here, is as a light buttery roll filled with a fruity custard.

## MAKES 24 POFFINS

### For the filling
2 cups (475ml) milk
¾ cup (150g) sugar
1 teaspoon vanilla extract
Pinch of salt
5 tablespoons cornstarch
6 egg yolks
1 cup (150g) berries of
   your choice

### For the dough
1 cup (235ml) water at 110°F
   (40°C)
2 (¼oz/7g) packets active
   dry yeast
½ cup or 1 stick (112g)
   butter, melted
¾ cup (150g) sugar
3 eggs
Food coloring, of your choice

1 teaspoon salt
4½ cups (540g) flour, plus
   extra for dusting
Egg, whisked, for washing
White sesame seeds,
   for sprinkling

1. First, make the filling. In a medium saucepan, bring the milk, sugar, vanilla extract, salt, cornstarch, and egg yolks to a boil, whisking constantly.

2. Reduce the heat slightly and continue to boil for a couple minutes. Stir constantly and make sure to scrape into the corners of the saucepan.

3. Take the saucepan off the heat and plunge into an ice-water bath to stop the eggs cooking further. Set aside to cool completely.

4. Now make the dough. Combine the water and yeast in a mixing bowl and let stand for 5 minutes.

5. Stir in the butter, sugar, eggs, food coloring, and salt. Add the flour, 1 cup at a time, and beat in.

6. Cover the dough with plastic wrap and refrigerate for at least 2 hours.

7. Preheat the oven to 375°F (190°C) and line a baking pan with parchment paper.

8. Turn out the dough onto floured surface and divide into 24 pieces. Roll each piece into a ball shape.

9. Add the berries to the custard filling and stir in. If you are using larger berries or fruit, such as strawberries, cut them into smaller pieces first.

10. Take one ball of dough at a time and press down on it to flatten it slightly.

11. Spoon about 1½ teaspoons of the custard filling into the center of each roll.

12. Pull up the sides of the dough and fold them over the filling, making sure each ball is completely sealed. You may need to wet your fingers to create a good seal. To be extra safe, put the ball sealed side down when baking.

13. Mold the dough into the Poffin shape and repeat for each piece of dough.

14. Let the Poffins rest somewhere warm for 25–30 minutes.

15. When done resting, put the Poffins onto your parchment-lined baking sheet.

16. Brush the Poffins in egg wash and sprinkle sesame seeds on top of each one.

17. Loosely cover the baking sheet with aluminum foil, to prevent browning, and bake for about 17 minutes, or until firm.

# INSPIRED BY SOUTH PARK
# CHOCOLATE SALTY BALLS

It might be debatable whether *South Park* is really "geeky," but I think the show has earned a lot of geek cred over the years with detailed references to such definitively geeky things as *World of Warcraft*, comic books, and *Star Trek*. *South Park* is generally not a good source of fictional food inspiration, as most of the satire is based in the real world and the show tends to aim for gross rather than appealing, but there is one exception: Chef's Chocolate Salty Balls.

Chef, voiced by the late Isaac Hayes, was the portly and promiscuous cafeteria cook for the first ten seasons of the show. As one of the more kind and down-to-earth characters, his advice was often sought by the four protagonists...though his advice generally manifested itself in totally inappropriate and non-relevant soul songs. This recipe comes from one of those humorously misguided soul songs, probably the most popular song from the show, titled "Chocolate Salty Balls." The song basically describes a recipe for a salty spherical chocolate pastry to...suck on. Despite the obvious metaphor here, I thought a salty spherical chocolate pastry sounded pretty darn good, and I was right! Chef's balls are delicious!

## SERVES 4–5

Butter or nonstick spray,
   for greasing
⅔ cup (150g) salted butter
1½ cups (150g) sugar
¼ cup (60ml) brandy
4 cups (700g) semisweet
   chocolate chips, divided
2 teaspoons vanilla extract
4 eggs
1½ cups (180g) flour
½ teaspoon baking soda
2 tablespoons ground cinnamon
½ teaspoon table salt
Coarse sea salt, to taste,
   for dusting

1 Preheat the oven to 325°F (170°C) and grease a baking pan.

2 In a saucepan, add the butter, sugar, and brandy and bring to a boil, stirring constantly. Remove from heat.

3 Using a wooden spoon, stir in 2 cups (350g) of the chocolate chips until melted. Remember to give that spoon a lick!

4 Allow the mixture to cool slightly, then stir in the vanilla extract.

5 In a large mixing bowl, beat the eggs until combined. Gradually add the slightly cooled chocolate mixture and mix well.

6 Combine the flour, baking soda, cinnamon, and salt, then gradually add this mixture to the chocolate mixture.

7 Stir in the remaining chocolate chips and spread the mixture into the baking pan.

8 Bake for 35–45 minutes, or until a fork inserted in the center comes out clean. Be careful not to burn your balls!

9 Let the mixture cool just enough so that it won't burn your hands. Meanwhile, set up a small plate or cutting board with some of the sea salt on it.

10 Scrape up the brownie mix, working around the edges—you don't want to use the hard edges for these balls.

11 Begin shaping rough 1-inch (2.5 cm) balls out of the mix, then roll them in the salt. Do this very lightly—a little sea salt goes a very long way.

12 If you do happen to oversalt, just brush off the excess crystals. Too much salt is bad, mmmkay? When you're done, put 'em in your mouth and suck 'em!

# ACKNOWLEDGMENTS

Rolanda Conversino, Mom, thank you so much for always thinking I'm awesome at everything. If everyone thought I was as great as you do I would probably be supreme master of the universe by now. You literally shed blood, sweat, and tears for this book and I am forever grateful for that. To your husband, Joe Conversino, thank you for letting me make a mess in your kitchen!

Thanks to my big brother, Nicholas Reeder, for teaching me to cook and making me like it. You're an all-knowing culinary mastermind that I can always rely on for answers and suggestions.

My family: your obsession with food rubbed off on me and this happened!

So much love for my best friend and soon-to-be husband, Jeff Diza, for driving me all over the place for ingredients, weathering my mental breakdowns, and for taking care of our little flock. You were there when I first had this wacky idea and you encouraged me to follow through. Your misguided but unwavering faith in me has helped me to have some marginal faith in myself.

Jessica Rausch and Wesley Garcia, thank you for being my quality-control minions! Jess, we were the ultimate fangirls in our formative years, weren't we? I think, like the butterfly effect or a water droplet on Laura Dern's skin, I might never have started *Geeky Chef* if I hadn't met you.

Kyle Cyree, your experience and advice when it comes to making and drinking alcoholic beverages was invaluable. Thank you for being such an awesome boss, you have helped me immeasurably on both a personal and professional level.

Amanda and Brian Backur, thank you for taking the time to test some of these recipes for me and giving me such great feedback. I can't wait to meet little Beowulf!

Thank you to my evil twin sister, Cassandra Rabini, for being a sounding board for my mom while she looked for typos and grammatical errors. And for watching *The Lord of the Rings* with me thirteen times.

Thanks to Denis Caron, for designing my amazing new logo, which I adore so much, and taking in stride my flights of whimsy and ever-changing mind in regards to the creation of said logo.

Thank you to Michael Molina, for always having awesome ideas to share with me and for always boosting my ego when I'm down on myself. I will see you again one day, I swear.

Thank you to Jeannine Dillon, for finding my little blog in the gigantic mess that is the Internet and making this book happen! Also, thank you to the marketing team for being so supportive!

To my readers, old and new: First of all, thank you for existing. You are such a great group of geeks.

I hope this book helps you make many wonderful and delicious memories!

To everyone else I love, hopefully you know who you are and thank you for tolerating me!

# ABOUT THE AUTHOR

Cassandra Reeder is an experienced blogger, avid home cook, and lifetime geek. For over six years she has been helping other geeks all over the world make their fictional food fantasies come true at www.geekychef.com. Cassandra currently lives in San Francisco with her husband and pet parrot. She has not yet trained her parrot to say, "Help me, I've been turned into a parrot!" but she's working on it.

# INDEX

134